The Derbyshire Poems

Also by Peter Riley:

Poetry
Love-Strife Machine
The Canterbury Experimental Weekend
The Linear Journal
The Musicians, The Instruments
Preparations
Lines on the Liver
Tracks and Mineshafts
Ospita
Noon Province
Sea Watches
Reader
Lecture
Sea Watch Elegies
Royal Signals
Distant Points
Alstonefield
Between Harbours
Noon Province et autres poèmes
Snow has settled ... bury me here
Author
Passing Measures: A Collection of Poems
The Sea's Continual Code
Aria with Small Lights
Alstonefield (extended edition)
Excavations
A Map of Faring
The Llŷn Writings
Greek Passages

Prose
Two Essays
Company Week
The Dance at Mociu

The Derbyshire Poems

Peter Riley

Shearsman Books
Exeter

First published in the United Kingdom in 2010 by
Shearsman Books Ltd
58 Velwell Road
Exeter EX4 4LD

www.shearsman.com

ISBN 978-1-84861-092-7

Copyright © Peter Riley, 1975, 1981, 1983, 2010.

The right of Peter Riley to be identified as the author of this work has been asserted by him in accordance with the Copyrights, Designs and Patents Act of 1988. All rights reserved.

Acknowledgements
The texts presented in this volume originally appeared in
Following the Vein (Albion Village Press, London, 1975),
Lines on the Liver (Ferry Press, London, 1981),
Tracks and Mineshafts and *Two Essays*
(both Grossteteste Press, Matlock, 1983).

Fourteen poems from *Tracks and Mineshafts* and eight poems from *Lines on the Liver* subsequently appeared in revised form in the 'King's Field' section of Peter Riley's *Passing Measures* (Carcanet Press, Manchester, 2000), as 'Material Soul', 'Prelude', 'Wandering Voices', 'Patina', 'Ballad of the Broken Bridge', 'Pause at Harecops', 'Driving down the Wye and Stopping', 'Driving up the Erewash and Arriving', 'Cavendish Cottages', 'No Sweet Dream', 'Distant Point', 'Greenwich Marshes and All the Way Home', 'Tumulus', 'Paws at Harecops', and poems 2, 3, 8, 11, 16, 17, 26 and 30 from 'Thirty Poems of Ten Lines'.

The author and publisher are grateful to Carcanet Press for their permission to include those poems in their original guise in this new edition.

Contents

Preface   9

Tracks and Mineshafts

I.
Material Soul   15
Eight Preludes   17
Kings Field   27
(two poems and a letter)   34
Glutton   38
(prose poem)   45
Pure Dread   46

II.
(a)
The light alternates...   49
Expert hero...   54
Wait for the light...   61
The flesh, skystruck   65
Year Cap split...   68
The Diatribe   69
Deeper into stone...   76
And there, at this very spot...   77

(b)
Held in conative energy...   81
The City's surface...   85
Flesh withstands...   87

(ending)
Adonaïs   89
And the miners...   90
The outside also matters   91

Lines on the Liver

1.
Spitewinter Edge Lookout Prose (untitled)   97
(a), (b), (c), (d/i), (d/ii), (e)

2.
Lines on the Liver: 30 poems   123

3.
Appendix: Processional and Masque (The Replies)   155

Following the Vein   165

Two Essays

Notes on Vein Forms   165
Theses on Dream   179

The Derbyshire Poems

Preface

These two books were first published in the reverse order of their conception and most of their writing: *Tracks and Mineshafts* by Grosseteste Press in 1983, *Lines on the Liver* by Ferry Press in 1981.

Tracks and Mineshafts was constructed from a lot of text written between 1978 and 1981, originally thought of as a work in the open-field mode concerning lead mining in the carboniferous limestone zone of Derbyshire and North Staffordshire. As a result of a conflict among different modes of documentation this was abandoned and what was rescued from it into the book was only what was clearly poetry, or a kindred kind of prose.

I see *Lines on the Liver* as a continuation, which begins by working its way quite laboriously through prose of hard thought, much of it still related to the "mining" scenarios of *Tracks*. I sometimes think I could have rendered these chunks of declaration and inquiry more attractive by attributing them to a collection of fictitious imams and rabbis, or a debate of Orthodox monks in some monastery hanging on the side of a cliff like cubist swallows' nests—"And the Archdeacon Vesuvius said…" etc. Anyway, the first-person singular hammering its way towards daylight through this section is finally released into short diurnal poems, a process which is continued in *Ospita* (1987) and the poems of *Snow has Settled...* (1997) in pursuit of more structured verse.

When 14 pages from *Tracks and Mineshafts* were included in the selection *Passing Measures*, published by Carcanet in 2000, they were all given titles and varying amounts of revision took place. The purpose of this was that they should stand alone out of their original context, as poems. In the present volume these texts have mostly reverted to their original states. No decision was ever made in the writing of the second part of this book as to whether the text on any one page was necessarily one poem, as against two or more small poems, or part of a poem, or no poems at all.

The changes that have been made to both books for this edition are mainly for the sake of verbal improvement, which amounts conceptually to little more than the correction of spelling mistakes.

The three poems of *Following the Vein*, published in an earlier version by Albion Village Press in 1975, clearly belong with the other material printed here. They were the first to be written and were completed much later, in a mode of symbolising the human form which I couldn't have extended into the larger works.

The *Two Essays* were published by Grosseteste Press as an appendage to *Tracks and Mineshafts* "to elucidate some of the imagery of the poems" in material and immaterial terms respectively, but they obviously ran beyond this purpose.

If anyone were to suggest that my use, in any of these works, of imagery of underground mining or of natural underground process in a discourse of the human spirit invoked "the unconscious" I would have to disagree. As far as I am concerned the process engaged is that of work, including the labour of coping with the subcutaneous mechanisms of the human body which empower exteroception.

Peter Riley,
Cambridge, April 2010

TRACKS AND MINESHAFTS

I

Material Soul

GIVEN TO death and life, no choice,
fallen into these terms, borne as the
tide bears the wave to its strike,
cut to bedrock, crest, charge the shore.
Given to this, life carving itself out
of its knowledge and the earth
is a cup to which the lip fits,
and the senses' final construct moves
relentlessly through substance to the houses
of light, mutual devotion

joined to death; danger
specifies its fear, the message forms
its own access or nerve and behind
the point of contact perception opens
onto a cleared space, a settlement, holding
people of all ages together,
the whole of life, is this shift
back, this rearing

and arrival, which leaves a mark,
a birth documentation or yell echoing
down the unlivable corridors and arcades
of transitional time. Flesh scores lines
in the calcium slag of earth and the spirit
wakes, the needle enters the groove,
polar tension shakes the circuit, which
responds, gapes, tremors, issues
forth into the acts of day, for good.
Peace is nothing without this resistance,
engaging distance beyond any possible
repair to the end, the inhabited city.

And this is what we see, and live, all round us the world arrives at its end. Welcome it, plunge into the stone, never to be seen again.

Eight Preludes

i

Each day some further light each day some farther dark.
Carry on go here there make a note of it what for.
Climb the hill walk down get in the car and drive away.
It is nothing to do with me. Valley stream
meadow waterfall gorge. There is something else there
nothing to do with us, that makes no difference.
We can go we can stay at home and drink tea, it is
still there. Far reaches of the Upper Manifold, where
is it, what is it, green chapel if it rains it rains.
Smear of cloud in the distance, book of nothing not
inhabited, ruins of the whole thing. Light on water
quick by blue shale cliffs, thick in fern, light filling,
bearing the vocabulary of a curved lack. Mineral vein
running down the hillside up the other side and away
over the moors, worked or not. Or not worked, unknown,
what difference does that make? Light filling the valley
with not a soul to be seen, dark beams of disappointment
filling the city streets, death shadowing the grass.
What am I then as you which otherwise stays sleeping, or
if we weren't in the dark star's way would our sense
still open beyond the ground whether we knew it or not?
No, the material soul yearns by the day's annoyance for real.
So does love in silver boxes hence dispatch our joyful stake
and I turn us again, front to front to front.

ii

Night outside is the theatre of our patience
as you lie beside me in the dark loft;
distant thrust of steam locomotive in some
vast marshalling yard, cold papers blown
across the square.

Night contracts the distances of love and fortune
to a presence, angles filling the dark room
loud with inaudible instructions like an
equestrian statue in the full moon and a far away
telephone rings.

It is me trying to contact a third person
out of the past or lost in the city streets while
night's cover persists—footsteps of the heart agent
passing by ticket office and clock tower
to an abandoned station.

Then false dawn brings a nil invoice and faint lines
near the ceiling, a small child runs down the corridor
holding a toy angel, wings flapping screaming at us
not to owe—the world is wanted, and full, our full hearts
crack at it.

And famine of the earth in pictorial wars, false
tensions, monetarisation of time whereas the emptiness
is real and there is no return, no restitution
oh keep intact the underwing starts, the
cup through it.

iii (a)

A sense of urgency and the kitchen floods. Most of the time gets mislaid.

The weekdays pass to the side; called to the present we wind ourselves up and something quite remote comes out: old jazz, demolished cafés where we breakfasted in our prime, a head full of grey mornings, quick postcards, old thorns . . . What time do I have to get up tomorrow?

Most of the time belongs to most of the people but I can't hear you, I can't find you, hero of our time, toy of our governors, I can't read you, I can't hear you for the grinding of milk-teeth, bone against bone, teeth chewing teeth in the cavernous half-light of a bottling shop . . . Hero of the double white line, humanity brought to the idea of itself, dying of imputative success, chewing itself to image pulp and anyway, when will a human idea ever eat real raisins or hold my hand on the way to the station when the time comes for questions? Every time it rains I know a nation is a logarithm of love, how the present tangles itself in desires, how the mess we make of it unwinds into space.

iii (b)

Snap. There is a reason
why discomfort gains the route.
The honey drips but the fire
leaps: be held out.

iii (c)

The reasons are all eaten in secret
or baked into Easter buns.
Superfluous honey corrodes
the map. We spit out pips
and fragments of grindstone
into the fire.

iii (d)

Thin liquids! give us some
annals of the orchard,
some fire laden rob.

iv

By the worm in the sky, by instruction,
the people would enter the state due them?
Unless otherwise stated it is a phantom dispatch.

Our wires live and respond; high gritstone kerbs
energy which isn't ours: we intersect, recognise
and worry. How we worry—darkness is

Two things and one of them (ness) is light
cutting through us. No rest, no tuition,
enter the island state guided in twain.

v

I am constantly bugged by something I think I'm supposed to be saying: the philosophy of poetry or the joys of wisdom or the truth that snaps the world back into place. Where is it? It's easy enough to focus on nothing like a missing pilot and set absence in the text just to have it there before us, newly reflective; but you are *elsewhere* and it's very uncertain that something human is actually there at the end of this dispersed line wanting or waiting for anything on earth. Surely the fire is getting low; if we don't signal our love there will be no reason for dying. I turn to the simple sky-trapped animal, the *looke in they heart and write*, bit. Plentiful and expensive. The heart, of course, is a nonexistent book in which we read the education of the world. The adventures of Bugs Hunter. What rubbish. *I am not I, pitie the tale of me.*

Meanwhile, someone is stockpiling sugar in an abandoned theatre across the road from where we live, and the cat returns for her dinner. Give it her, naturally. We can't turn back at this stage. Open her tin, welcome her children behind the couch, find them as good homes as time and this world afford. These necessary acts compose one by one the map of grace. Everything glows with sheer presence: couch, kittens, bugs, boredom, dark, ness, it all slowly gathers to a landscape, an inhabited and structured landscape with walls and ditches and paving by which we hold on to the world like a vast hand. And that also is love, whose grip, routed into purpose, steadies us against the earth exactly here: dispersing in our heat but consolidated by fear, the tension of the wing, that opens and closes. What wing? What rubbish again. Opposite the theatre of sugar a wing of rubbish opens to our esteem.

vi

Willing also to be remembered, lost
in fairest love-task scholarships such
as bring sight to its own predilection
where the broken edges catch the light
unfolding, a tract where sense
and love fuse in the energy of script
holding the world together at that point.

And immense wastage, entirely ours
as we humanise the world and then resent it
objectify it and wonder where it's gone
and place such clamps on our speech that
most of the people become figments of something
shot past like a disintegrated pudding too late for
winter, lost in clouds of fume.

But I also think of you as fairest before sight
in a vocabulary which is generally considered
nonsense out of a 13th Century context and still
fairer dark by the light that glims beyond.
Well, it is night at the crossroads and many years
since a dignitary came this way. The faces
of the houses are silent. Time suddenly rusts.

vii

Faint calls from the mines,
intrusive holes in the landscape
or star targets.

Of the heart of the earth
where the one-person is undivided
and the market serves the home.

Of the oceanic cycles
where the dream disperses into day
and we cannot rest in our value.

Of the self cast.

viii

If you want messages you must provide an orifice.
But to really want messages is in itself an orifice,
a lesion, an interruption of the diurnal pact. The future
ferments in this cleft, packed with honour and disdain,
drawing us ever larger and further on, to this self-
same world, that listens; the rest is vain stuff.

Surely it is this whole particular, this action we
are that draws our sight into the funnel, opening
and closing as the light wing flutters, back
and forth, back and forth, wisdom and rubbish—
poetry is the flight. And now if I can just get out
of this notional claw I'll find out exactly where I am.

>   I'm in the dining shed again exactly up and about
>   my morning task I crawl at this morning through
>   the floss of dream. In a wink I fill the kettle
>   and forget it. I shake the radio. I wince.
>   The light outside is clearer than any hypothesis.
>   The edge resounds in light because we don't linger.
>
>   And off to work I go. I enter a solid block
>   of morning light scored with branch lines;
>   I close the door before you even wake, check
>   ignition and brakes and turn again to the book,
>   to the page shewn, the passage marked before.
>   Fate, it says, is a professional improvisor.

I duck under the brow as the overtakers
glide past in their dream wagons: Monday
Tuesday and Wednesday, fleeces thick in oil.
Feeling "rushed" (like "crowded") mounts to
a signal. I turn into a lay-by with herbage. Rain
clouds the stream. The entire landscape is vocal.

I lean on the parapet while the police matrons
check my documentation, and listen to the story
of the water vole, his home under the bridge, the pain
of his extended incisors. He breathes under Saturn
and scurries along the bank. He eats or is taken—he
knows that. His duties end at his honour to himself.

We have considerable doubts, but raise a song
of this inadequacy the thrush couldn't fault.
And we keep it, chuck it over the shoulder for
luck and resume direction. A mended stone.
Nothing any longer bears on us that isn't ours;
nothing any longer wears us that isn't love.

Hell in some century's language is where no one
makes a life any more. We have the key to it, fast
to the wrist under the sleeve, the misplaced heart.
Then we mine into light in a way no office can
endure or regulate save the office of delight,
past and future safe in a shell and love's farther still.

King's Field

Patches of bare earth on the far hillside: abandoned mines, standing out like sores through the rough mingling pastoral surface—scorched by the core of the earth as by a passing meteor. Sites of encounter, engagement, victory and defeat, where a piece of nature split against humanity, into metal and slag.

Teeth marks on the shoulder and flank of the hill, scatter of clinker in the grass, compacted rain-washed mounds glittering with small surfaces of calcite and quartz . . . The craftsmen of fire departed long ago, decamped and returned home under the sunset in a dying wake of mineral flame: the fire they inhabit, and work with, treading the bright coals, walking the furnaces . . .

Earth substance and sky energy converged at Man, wedged in the point of creation, nuclear cocoon, handling the living gold, fixed moaning on the rock . . .

Until the work is completed and past, and we hold the result in our hands and our everyday perceptions, and the whole process, in retrospect, becomes an instant, a flash of penetrating fire—the book, closed, becomes one thing, the coinage fused to a crown.

Leaving us here bewildered, leaving us with a cold in the throat and a mass of sterile rock at our feet and no idea what to connect living to, no continuing occasion or ferial relief; leaving us holding a medallion against the moon, stamped with cold royalty.

As if the present is something already lived.

As if we could pick what we think we want out of the
world leaving behind the hole we dug it from, let the
rest fall aside, without getting trapped in a speed tank
of proliferating division, where sympathy is merely
the recourse against a massive dispersal of substance
and love strains against income to keep a few people
together in true lives. We are outside ourselves: we have
no architecture.

It is dangerous, for the world returns us to ourselves in the end,
in the formats of our own acts—intimately, eventually,
the world has us as we have had the world. Right through
the boundaries of our estates the world splits back at us,
returns our vocabulary ground to a knife edge while the
residue crumbles and shakes over our heads.

As if it were possible to gain the run-off from the treaty
of stone and fire as a bystander, to make or continue
anything without inhabiting the generative point, the
ecstasy, and bearing its toll. As if our hoarded sentences
were anything but paper hedges against the expanse,
excuses for lateness and silence, thorn collars for the
refusal to say.

And we hold on, fingernails tight in the engravure, as the
bounty of the original act disperses through the years
into cloudy smears of gardenage. Nettle, willow-herb
and bindweed creep up to the mouth of the mine,
smothering the work floors and smelt holes. Smoke
and gauze float in the air, blotting the earthscape. It has
always been like this.

Now as probably at any other place in history the trophies
seem to be secreted, the currency reserved. Indolence and
jealousy pull us down, we fill with disappointment, time
resentment, struggling in blatant hypocrisy to survive
on input without living any real events at all, just a few

token games, bitter takings we never worked for. It is the language that fails.

The language lapses, families cooling and drifting apart, bitterly shrugging each other off, emotional victims of regressive economics, taking a shabby single room in a Victorian terrace to live through the clouding of the mirror, withdrawal of speech down the throat. Twist of flex in a circlet of yellow plaster-work, old carpet, naked bulb, dusty settee draped in Indian shawls: anything, a few bits and pieces, a cold fire. Work discontinued and disproved in the lost kitchen, victims of metallic ambition: experience lived as instant coin.

So there is a void section, a wastage, which can't be reprocessed back to possibility. Ice cracks the shell and cups the seed; the faintest reminder of participation floors us. All sense of belonging is suspended, "Purity of heart is to will one thing" but no extant script will recover the retrospective simplicity, the lost whole.

Leave things aside then for a term, attend to the present, the one thing. Go shopping, write a letter, go to the cinema, the art of forgetting. Ruthlessly adhere to normality as it stands at any price, sharpen senses to the weather, that alternate freezing and melting we get on the edge of North, water always running down the fields, and the world is just what you see.

And sharpened to that edge, non-claimant, totally engaged in the substance of living and the thought that survives it, we begin to recall ourselves, brought home from distance and obscurity with always some 'wholeness' behind us, whole because behind us, which the world casts back in our faces as marginal loss and we dream from every night. But the only real thing is here in the hand that holds it: life focused on points of distinction.

To meet this demand a flame is held back in the eye.

There are points of light all over the valley, where the sun catches car tops greenhouses and puddles, piercing the winter haze filling the air—a body of light gathered piecemeal towards us and held there, suspended, animate light, between us, that anyone should be glad to die into as it throngs up and over and soars on the horizon, beckoning the night.

Casually we brush it off with excuses, headaches and liabilities, crushing the distance between us, the caution zone, to a slight thing—you and I, descend the stone steps in the hillside and pass under cloud into the real, where things also clasp and contain the light, have it in substance, and the objects of earth stand in absolute presence through light and dark, holding energy close and ripe, solid, with nothing needing to be said.

Finally the person, redoubled in native fire: animal combustion but also the tip of flame held in our good-will, illumination of the heart page in a dark cell at night, to which all that cosmic display bows: the human warmth that splits the rock and melts out the copper and gold, commingling, consuming our bodies... Flame that gains as it disperses, consolidates and augments as it flares on the horizon the blue lettering of anyone's few, accurate, sentences... And the more we distribute the more we hold, the more we tell the more we know.

Then the sun is safe in the sky and the hills well wrapped in grass and bushes, with outcrops and bare patches where the human and divine construct spat a brief statement to the ground, or bit a chunk out of the hillside. The people of the town stroll around on a bright afternoon, their protean potentials well concealed in human casing, formative / caustic energy more or less deeply packed in travelling suitcases of flesh and bone, occasionally breaking out in sparks of meaning that flash across the circuit, while a constant pressure slowly moulds and consumes the active surface of the person—

This ferment in us, that belongs nowhere else, and is the force that moves us anywhere, forming mere distance into resounding arcades and terraces, lakes, rings, graveyards ... and is certainly not at home in these lumpy sacks, walking bolehills with no fixed site in the world, fighting constantly with shoelaces tape-recorders and each other in search of a rightful being or a wrongful reward; and harbouring all the time a perceptive nux that in true response opens out to gardens and edging woods, creates the world and belongs nowhere in particular.

Human body gurgling and rattling in its excess of language, that stands between us and the source of life as our only access, ditheringly in the way between the self and its permanent home: final pivot and moment of peace that must be all body, all nothing at all.

Don't we already know it and as if in preparation are brought constantly up against the ordinary things, that signal personal redundancy, the mass of the earth in its hideous simplicity that alone gives energy and light any substance or durability, where language crashes and revives, flesh reconstitutes itself athwart times. It is the message that exceeds us, the concept not grasped, the emptiness of total being, pure sign of itself to which such substances as metal, poetry history, can only form the tools of an interim script. Immovable and unspeakable, the mournful dump of matter ...

What can we do but set the fire through it, immediately and rightly adore the quick glitter of roadside glass as a sign of hope. For truth swells in the very instant we live it, holding sheer surfaces out to catch the soul-fire, burning seed, candlelight still as standing water under its technological canopy, waiting to lapse into the world space of a specific attention, kept alive through millennia, simple openness of response to authentic script, across wars and famines.

What if that too, upper sense of the heart furnace, in the end fails, scatters and dies into featureless geology? What if that too breaks its percepts against the things of earth, that nullify all our languages and strategies: the friendly local object which is also the death of culture, the utterly unbroachable world-thing lying there sucking endeavor towards nonentity—the stone in the field, the light bulb, the rusty stapler, the terracotta head dripping with chicken blood and wine ... These things we have given our lives to and they finally sit there on the desk staring back at us entirely void of expression or promise, unsellable untelling exhibits, tools that we have set at the focus of increment and exhausted—vehicles of intercommunication from which we expect oracles. And we batter our spirits against the grey matt surface, the screen that now refuses to cast back either spring blossoms or infant smiles. We are reduced to knots of hair and gristle at the crossing point of human and cosmic wills, wide open to the annihilating denials of infinity. Of course we are, and always knew it.

And still the authentic embodiment of light playing to and from the world remains celestial whether it lasts or not, still in its torn jacket this globe of thinking flesh is the song of it, the new star mounting the rinsed and morning sky, fresh from ocean, shrouded in its own time. It notifies the successor and warns the sleeper, tracing an arch across the firmament, and finally descending to its dim repose: the true moment thwarted against unbearable extent, and in painful response echoing back the form of a spiritual figure, full of beauty. The talk of the town.

Completely answering the world.

(Sacred phosphorus inside his
small head, cloaked in
snow & humus, clock intact. Brain-

glow holds morning in reserve, its own
and not the echo of any received light:
we wake up because the dream is exhausted

and falls through the slot in the door
in little bits. Likewise
we receive the day's failure
into our bed at night.

This perseverance
and fellowship with separation
operates a quite different economy
from what shows on th'electronic
balance-sheet at
recking time.

The light (this
morning) falls out of the sky
and passes into the ground
and the stone and slate of the roof

falls into heat
and number
at substance, where
shadows contrive

and the rising penumbra
intercepts
this divine speed
ay, at the forge of lives.

(Letter)

Yes, you have needed to distance, unmask, normalise. You are no longer held in that relentless intensity, your pitch has dropped and spread, you are not focused on a redemptive centre at the point of decision, yours or another's. I think it is important to know that this, your state of being, is only the occasion of what you do (your writing, your work) and not its substance. It was a 1960s confusion from which many received lasting damage, to think your fate would respond to a conditional, shorn of act. And I don't see why this recovery, which is what it is, has to be represented as some kind of failure. Welcome in fact to the world, where you go on, and the double-edged images no longer cut the heart, and objects no longer (fencepost, omnibus, feather, crystal) recede. Things stay more to your side, completing. And so you move on, past the defeated and defeating questions of who you are by reflection and accession; you move to a wider, more social, and apparently firmer sphere. And it makes no difference at all—nothing changes—the blood does as much flow, the meat pulse, as much hurt as much comfort as ever, as much confusion. Whoever you are the red string dangles at your centre, don't deny it—you are no longer hurt, but hurt remains in your sense, the demand persists and pays no attention to our smooth adulthoods and their reckless persistence. The formal energies of our constitution transcribe such urgencies as reach us, drawing them to a linear journal, which is a twisted and coarse but final means of having done with it. The intensity may be the way but it is not the message; the message is less particular (who it has) and more exact: the whole sphere of singularity has to support the flashes and sediments it receives under command to finish as known truths. Whatever it is (firestick, handlebar, dictionary, sea) that bears and threatens it, this craft won't be tied to selected personal qualifications of youth race temperature or history, which flaw the very singular authenticity of the structure. Surely the whole of life is the issue at every point by obtension—your crisis is a metaphor—you are focused (scissors, maypole, tumulus, gun) on a redemptive centre.

Glutton

Grey limestone ridge under transverse sweep of low cloud, full of cavities, crystals, and men sharpened to a point.

•

Minerals come slowly to fruition, across millennia: molecules of lead and sulphur riding air-bubbles in the warm waters pouring and seeping between masses of solid limestone, coming to flower under the roof of hell. The metal trends westwards and upwards, final outcast of an oceanic pulse rising towards the atmosphere. This bright thread worms its way towards the sky along borderlines and faults in the tables of sleepy limestone, round the corner, skirting and infiltrating the vast shell-dust annals: solidified white powder full of crinoids and molluscs, blocks of pure defence. A line, then, compounded of metal, oil, and heat, traces the edges of sedimental stasis and sets up a challenge on the edge of contentment. It approaches, fastened to weightless air; it is held up to us. It glows in the subterranean night, calling us, persuading us to faster and sharper acts—a tight, iridescent vein packed with sleeping princesses and red thorns ...

•

Approaching the surface of the earth, this perilous band curves back on itself, sheltered by the white rock. Gaining cavities, cracks and entire vacant layers of the stratification, it opens out into efflorescences: crystals and cave-pearls, colours of sky and flesh held in translucent stone, breaking into the spaces in formal excrescences. The metallic compound lies amassed at the centre of the cauldron. It is as if a whole warehouse of books lies under the sea, the books stacks on their sides; the pages congeal together, the languages forgotten, cubic masses of documentation totally inert. But the gilt letters one by one float off the bindings and assemble on the surface in a matrix of red and blue inks, a dazzling unreadable scum, a potentiality. And waits there, as if expecting us, an ore. Always referred to as "true", the nascent language is there, and ready, as soon as our organs of perception are tuned to meet it.

•

Men sharpened to a point plunge into the earth. Flesh breaks out into hooks and probes, teeth focus in tight clusters like poppy heads. They grope in water-rooms, labyrinths, hotels with bricked-up windows, bank vaults, scenes of lust and criminal heat scored onto the walls, a whole fresco of despair. It is a desire constantly renewed, a driving force only marginally attached to gain—impersonal and irrevocable, pure species act. Men goaded to nerve heat twine with the dragon in ecstasis of parity. Set around with guard mechanisms, channelled, under command, the miner's eye catches a lustre, a hidden spark in the tensed rock which fires his anonymous souldom and he sets to, blow against blow, hunter under his moon. Pressed and focused into this encounter anyone's wholeness is broken and rephrased like a larva in the chrysalis. Care is elbowed aside and behind in the fray, becoming the function of an over-language and progressively eroded as ever more refined instruments of penetration release perception from direct engagement. But by then the metal is exhausted too.

•

So like anyone going a lonely walk, head down against the blast, dog trussed up alongside, snow on the valley sides and steam in his pockets, the destruction and sterility wrought by taxonomy stands always before him as a possible channel for his acts. There is no message for the world, there is not even any news. Scales and inscribed plates fall off his spirit into corners as he wrenches his life out of a stone vice or crumples in the attempt. Fighting the globe for the faintest sign of ore, stuffed in a niche under the fields with barely room to turn round, his work-focus becomes such complete anti-home, so specifically unwelcome, that the rest of the world, the width of day, brightens in response behind him in a fury of tears. A wholeness burgeons out of sight, in front beyond the rock, behind in the day, language of a royalty he doesn't himself in his moment speak, but works for. Life is sectioned—greatest pleasure in the sweep of earth's width now stands against an alternated blindness and rage, from which it catches a melancholy renunciation, a funereal suspension. The sweep of light across the land is caught in the cone of night and directed against the rock-face. You stand at the shouldering of this structure or nowhere.

•

And attains the unfeared present (tomorrow) cap in hand, open past the crux to full orbit, folded in night and secretly aglow.	The future, you see, no longer simply "arrives". It is or is not an improvement; tomorrow's daylight is clearly already there.

•

It is a matter, then, of bringing this tension, this long curve of time across the earth, this metallic arc, to a perfection it cannot gain itself, where the tightly compacted mass is broached at its bud and its flower is released into the active space of human society. The metal shoots out in pointed flames, casting off its earth; it is given birth to; its potentiality becomes an actuality; it shouts through the land. Twined metal thread corkscrews up the spine, gold emblazonry on the canopy, coins and nails. It leaps and spans its cyclic course, and falls back to earth, recombines with its sulphide and runs pell-mell to the sea.

•

Raising the question of whether it is we that are using the metal or the metal that is using us ... Steel works closes with loss of 2000 jobs.

•

Man wound up to a knot of muscle, all fixed eye and lung, blind and deaf to the spreading world, stabbing and pecking at the ore, tearing it down, owl-man, hawk-man, man in despite of himself, driven into an underground language-laboratory by the ache in the clay and hammering at a proposition until it yields its full and proper sequel with all the arts of war ... Man at his worst, focused entirely on the one point of engagement with the world, deaf and dumb to all the rest of the year. The only consequence he accepts is the immediate gratification. The shining stuff tumbling into the box.

•

But he brings it down, he wins it, and refills the hole in time with the residue. A position is moved to a result, a work is completed, and passes out of his hands into distribution and coinage, not his concern. And he returns, day after day he returns to the workface, year after year until there is nothing left worth getting, the cavities in the hill are scraped clean and everything else is sunk in water beyond reach. The latch on the door rusts into nonentity or disappears beneath stalagmite while the door fades into a fungus-stain. His work encapsulates his death somewhere deep in the head of a casual historian or local hobbyist, strolling over broken ground. He disdains secondary pickings.

•

He continues always in the prime cause. He passes through narrow tunnels and vast slippery caverns in search of his love, following the twists and jerks of the vein, where it divides and re-forms, drawing yellow twine through his eyes by the pale flicker of his forehead on the blank walls, streaked red and brown like Sunday's dinner. Indeed everything homely is mercilessly parodied in these appalling underground routes and halls: an old mattress perched on a cavern ledge like an electronic clock at a chess match, relic of some earlier defeat, some troglodyte earnestness interrupted by the police; bits and pieces of homeland pressed everywhere into service as props and winches: parts of mangles, bed-ends and stair-rails coated in slime and flow-stone. The drowning of years moves under his feet. The palace of flesh is dark, silent, and smells of gunpowder.

•

Ruthlessly, ear-plugged, he delves for the true substance, the one result, bright and whole in the tray ready for processing into the world. It and its potential harm is then someone else's burden, but at least it is the real thing; whatever Society puts it to there is no excuse to be passed back to Nature: the material was initially true as delivered. He knows nothing about all that—diplomacy, "piecemealing", invasions of ore-bearing countries in the name of Freedom, bread bleached with white lead, self colonization, debased coin, screen illusions, enforced waste, cheap copper for the East India Company, echoic side-focus into nothing at all—he knows nothing of all that. Through the hollow climate of singularity he persists until there is no more, the metal bridges its last gap to the sea and the mines close. The reward remains in the sky for future workers: star headband last seen as a pale signature on a pardon: man's privilege, the blood-leap, joyous cap. He destroys himself.

•

He works at nothing but his own death. Only the constraints on him, only the worries, humanise or harmonise his career, opening it to a possible future, by the analogy of the tilled field. Customs and combinations lift his torn self from the pit and carry it back to his family.

•

The hill, the limestone ridge, is riddle with these abandoned courses, thousands of failures scarring the walls of tunnels and shafts—tracks of the spark, the minute speck of light at the bottom of the box he sank into. His entire life glows beyond his death, like everyone else.

•

Grey green limestone ridge seeming to brush the transverse sky heavy with cumulonimbus. In that narrow, hardly distinguishable band between the ridge top and the cloud is a wind-swept table-land littered with old furniture, crumbling headgear, forgotten shafts, tumuli, TV masts, telegraph poles, engine houses now barns, neglected greystone walling, broken ground with mounds, hollows, and crumbling banks. The soil rich in calcium encourages the growth of eyebright and dyer's greenweed. And in the failing but persistent light of day's end a grey aura everywhere as it all slowly sinks into bibliographic oblivion, closed and falling, faint murmur of traffic from the town below, scattered rooks in the air, tufts of wiry grass swept sideways ... How the whole band curves and storms into the valley shaking with lies and broken promises, the whole stratum scribbled and fought over and over and completely illegible, the lights below gasping supine for information-thrills, the town pulling the fringes of distance over itself, fighting for sleep. The wind battens the grass, beats and plunges about my head as the light finally slips away and the meaning of these paltry ruins is swept over the heads of the town and away, for really there is nothing to be gained from all this febrile perseverance and concentration, there is no linear reward and nothing is secured until death.

The world is missed, again and again, we are busy in a darkness while the days flew over us like birds in a storm and only the total sum of a life will show a moment's burgeon. Surely we catch the joy of it where this thread refolds on itself at love's conclusion.

A person's single reach continued to its end where it's fast to the earth possibly becomes in the back thrust and petalling of patience, becomes the shelter sited beyond this medium ground, death shining like a solid star, blasted through eternity and exclusively here as the line taut across hope is at that goodly moment inhabitable, and will be indefinitely.

•

This hollow globe is incapable of inaccuracy. Reward lines it. And at once the closed landscape wrapped in tough grass held tightly to the earth, our single star, is held among us as it slowly dawns on us, our prize is the earth.

Pure Dread

Green & white valley and the river
fast, double, manifold, always
full when most empty, bright threads
across the land, spring grass and
history it doesn't mean a thing
if you're sure to go.

Nightscape cast in space, patches of
white rock glowing in the fuzzy darkness,
questionless, clouded eyes turned aside
and why not when we get what we are in the
end anyway, always, end up with what
we are bound to.

Duple creature, quick river every summer
vanishing into the earth, to secret courses
and underground lakes, empty bed blazed up
the valley centre, pebbles hot to the hand.
Carry them up to the summit caves,
the ox-head wake.

In winter constant rush and throb of water against
stone, arch of sound, sides of night forming,
our eyelids are stapled to the earth,
we are guardless and empty without you,
plodding simply back to an unnoticed room,
eyelids stapled to the earth.

II

THE LIGHT alternates, comes and goes
in days and years and yet remains
the perfection of constancy held in
the length of terrain by human sight.
The streams descend from the hills
and meander over the plain, broadening
and deepening, receiving the sun's face
and casting it back onto the side walls
of old terraced houses, slowly decaying
factories, small hospitals, brick sheds
deep in bracken and willow-herb, sites
of persistence, signs that we are
here to stay, all of us, stations
whose weathering is on record
and anchors the language to a history
of completions.

Then there is nothing trustworthy in this world
but the heartfold, the construct that endures
beyond our means. Our promises are worth
less than the cheapest fastener on the market
and the earth falls away at a touch.
                                          The city—
the plastic spoon, the double bed, the book.
What else holds us, what sparkling trellis across
the race meaning a trust we don't actually
perform—of course it breaks—we know
perfectly well where social good resides,
at the journey's end, the making quest.

And deep in a diurnal faulting, wedged
into a space making both day and night seem wide,
someone is working, peering, scratching away,
and the lamplight of a den persists undimmed
for weeks, burning brighter and sinking deeper

into the gap between two homes, where man
in solitude delves at the bases of love,
the weight and stability of the transcript itself.

To see one thing clearly we distort
the entire landscape: it bends, clouds,
dissolves and slips away to a darkness
out of time; and the one thing being known
at once radiates back its own illumination,
splaying up the cleft towards day.

The landscape is fed back to its source
at our fingertips; the one thing being made
is hoisted up the shaft towards home,
redoubling the truth of what's there,
by what's surely somewhere

That we have as an idea of perfection, moving
with us on the earth in a strict veracity
to which the light responds, playing
and diversifying its facets among
the town roofs and windbreaks—
the realisation of potential articulated
into a document, the moral law delivered
from nowhere by an ancient child
who crawled out of a hole in the ground,
the simple tale of light on the fields

That spreads over the meadows and estates
every morning, rears itself aloft
and late in the day slides sideways away
off the pointed roofs and hedge backs
it flows, and slips away, never
(in a way) to return, since we are mortal.

And fail. Warp and crack like the earth;
we know what's right but the body is weak,
and shrinks in fear before the non-person,
the person nullified into command.
And there is probably some advantage in this failure,
something secret and speculative, unclear
to the self, likely to end in resignation
from event, work, world or sense.

    Stay with us! Get up! There is work to be done:
    the King is sick or sad, the cabbage patch
    is run riot and the ore lies under our feet.
    And none of these stands a chance without
    specific challenge, leverage, frontal focus—
    the moment is decisive, and slips ahead of us,
    disappearing into the flux.

The roundabout in the play-park
spins on, grey sky on the paving,
the rooks rise and swerve aside.
Suburban structures: colleges, workshops,
bungalows, horizontal slabs, ashamed
of their lack of detail—springs of the heart
held taut, nothing for the light
to engage. This empty success
spins on. There's no one near it.

"It is better to fail, and to fall short, than
to succeed as the non-person. But in failing,
and being defeated by all that vacant armour
you not only further the descent into bitterness
you also gain in your way some of the apparent
and immediate rewards of brutality: ease, self
reinforcement, the comfort of discomfort stifled.

"For goodness' sake aren't we defeated threatened
emptied enough by the world and our bodies not to add
to the store arguing with phantoms, tricks of air,
an empty suit, a manner—nothing there, nothing to be
afraid of, nothing to love. Waiting to be condemned
by an expert on heroes you don't trust, you end up
suspended on full pay. Congratulations."

EXPERT HERO Judge, Spirit of the Lamp sprouting
up from the space at the centre of the person—
he arrives in the night, uninvited and unexpected,
clears the table and starts examining the books.
No, he doesn't need a cup of anything thank you.
Page after page he prises open the weatherstones,
moths and maybugs hammering on the window panes,
he weighs our reluctance against metal and opens
the road into substance, that stretches as far
as anyone knows. And once the opening is known
someone has to go through it. If you merely play
at access the money turns to treacle.

Patriarchal, he speaks for and against us, alt-
ernates, shouts hope & failure from a stone box
in a tumulus until the sleepers can't sleep and someone
is sent out to deal with it, answer the world, Go—
Go we to seke that we shall nat fynde, the new lover
sets off in the grey dawn closing the earth
around him, pauses under the cold gatehouse to
adjust a shoulder strap, wipe a tear, enters
the wind and sticks out a thumb.

The captains of industry perceive
a roadside shadow, a flicker of darkness
against the wall. They all
head for the city.

Bone holds flesh in a cup
as does limestone, hold lead ore,
aloft, indeed up to us,
shielding the meniscus
against the weather with
a flat and bony hand. We inhabit
a concatenation—

Succession of barely noticed moments
which add up to the absolute conditional
of the person, something fixed beyond our
intervention as if it were a dream, a closed building
and the key is a bright idea somewhere
else, far away, behind a barrier. But
the barrier is alive, flesh, the barrier is us.
Which is only to say that it is difficult
to direct a life, and the heart thrives
on the fine detail at its constant centre—
the true moment at which we do have a leverage
on our existence, that holds the key, the code,
the cup of plenty to which everything turns,
the jewel of earth—

Here! Ordinary! Personal! Lived!
—new and immediately full response
set in its own discovery at the out-
come of tension and resistance:
the resolution that we seek somewhere
beyond its loss stands in front of us:
the one true thing, the life being
worked. Not the whole. The present
surety. And it is held up, and calls
out to us across the bleak shores and
engine shops of the land like
an infant cry, a note that sounds

slightly ahead of its striking
in an empty city.

And all the high set objectives
we read of in the whiteshell annals
are the dense core of nothing—
the object at the end of the tunnel
a calcium mantle, glowing erratically
in the cavernous half-light, fixed on us,
seeming to approach as we approach it,
straight before us. It must be
a distraction, it has to be a trick,
there's no one anywhere near it.

The metal reconstitutes its ore in the sad rain
and there is no enduring substance, this hard fabric
is nothing—a cloud under the moon, whirling ash,
crumpled and soggy paper in the middle of the road—
career-based decisions, uncaring circulars . . .

Oh bore it, pierce
that thick, insensate grin
to the quick, busy
flesh alive with distant light.

Every faint gesture rebounds on us
leaving a vacant hollow in the world:
possible, unfulfilled acts embedded
in the tissue, growth points too late—
the land is riddled with failed promises
and premature returns.

He picks his way among hollows and craters,
earth funnels of abandoned mineshafts,
bracken fields, rose bushes gone wild,
dry voices ringing in the air
exhortations to labour and be patient—
derelict electricity sheds, tram lines
sunk into gravel, grassed-over courts;
he passes rows of empty cottages,
inhabitants now hospice inmates,
boarded-up shops and brick-scattered streets,
chapels and hermitages in stony wastes
all empty, sites of development, reflex impact,
populations blasted to nonentity.

Sky-hatred, she said, has only one object:
you and I. That, then, is the prize—
accept cash, take no porous deferment,
bone illusions, phosphor worry tricks,
takeovers, price rises, cancer, hijacks . . .
The only substance broken and not severed
shared and not divided is love.

        Bolted fast in empty night,
        only a few pointers
        on the surface of event,
        lights on the quarry face we
        prise open: will
        the door open and
        she be there in
        her multifloral bodice?

As he passes up into the valley, a multiplicity
opens at the terminals of vision:
the earth horizon, full of bought things,
lit from beyond loved from within,
casting mental energy back on the liver
sufficient indeed to the single purpose of
living nobody could deny the one desire we
ever at the most are; and begin to multiply.

The future lies embedded in conglomerate
at an underground junction where fossils
seek revenge for our very enjoyment
of the world in all its days.

We can ignore it, and do, opting for elevation
but then the more of the world we scan
the more impossible monstrosities are revealed
until we bury our heads in travel like any tourist
and moan about the multiplicities of home.

And always the point of generation, turning
and dividing point, is there at the avid focus
where we fold our flesh round the blade:
total transmission. I mean death
joins us in hope.

And we can turn from failure
as from nourishment, se-
lect but not really, we are
not thieves.

We wait at the light,
we feed ourselves
to the unsevered gate,
the instrument.

WAIT FOR (each day) the light
feeding through the instrument
to emerge and fan out miles
above our heads, bearing
what we can't yet know
across the sky at speed
and leaving a faint moony glow
on our hands like a trace of dream
a February window scene
which broke under the drill
which spoke under the hill and was
carted off in lorry-loads to front a bank.

Late in its course the stream turns south
and courses to the equinox, free at last
of slopes and details it widens and deepens,
making its own way, picking up fragments
of human bondage, returning to source.

We spread our language through the world
laterally, drifting southwards, seeking warmth
as if unwittingly but not without hints
of requitement to the world at large against
an inner vacuum, blasting gold out of
native populations like so much dead rock.

Now her beams fall unmet to ash
in the lobby ashtray,
and puny sparks of hired spite
fall onto the map,
the world's table, obscuring
all the carefully sought detail
under scars and burns
of impersonated anger. It is handed
to the archivist.

Again the transcript is netted
under preservative (sorry of her
latent fear to be the ever bud)
and this is fairly well how we live.
It is more and more like the sky plane
rotted through with stars.

The sea, that great portrayal of the sky,
bounds right across the earth and smears
the local beach with shell paste, that
settles and hardens as the waves
steal slowly back. A residue, a vocabulary.

The fuzzily scanned future of our acts
becomes a chalky rubble under our feet,
crumbling downgrade, offer and result
of protection from climate, horizontal
bone web across the rim of hope, we
sink in it, to the ocean floor.

We mould the materials of earth to our own rhythms
ignoring the backlash—we sink into the ground.
The two-faced caretaker sleeps through a televised
transplant of which he is star victim, exchanging
his person for an image held in time, instant replay.

As if merely connecting the self
made your future, or anyone else's.

In the dim green light of an industrial chapel
the hero of this section eats Nottingham lace
at a seemingly endless presentation dinner.

Stay by me
distracted advocate,
alternating light
falling past me

        The hills and plains, river
        valleys, corners and quarters
        of the town, wrapped
        in early day—keep them
        free of our connections.

        Let them be what they are
        as the accountant hurries to work
        on a cold sunny morning, pulling
        his coat tighter at the neck
        as he rounds the demolition block,

        Dreaming of coffee or company
        and the narrower light in a shop window
        catches a gold ring (my father,
        Manchester c1935, wondering
        if he could afford to get married).

The flash, skystrike,
borrows me to air—
fruit never fully
accounted.

THE FLESH, skystruck,
burns me to air-fruit,
never finally accounted

and the faceless sky's face,
sharper than dawn, wider than day,
met in mid career as a bright, tensed,

slightly creaking surface casting back
the world as something suddenly *there*,
the danger that realises the fear,

at a touch flies open. The sky-mirror breaks
through us and the world behind it falls;
distance becomes total.

The blast shakes the hill, and caught
in the tunnel, facing the dragon head on,
the only defence is the point, hub of patience
      at the end of the sword

(The trick is to strike quickly
and dart ahead of the outcome,
then return for serious dealings.)

(Obviously anything coming towards you armed in a tunnel is the earth, the culmination of your doubt, whatever it is. Whether it's a member of the thought police or your lover's fading eye, it's still the earth, ash and streams, forests and hills, petrol stations and customs houses and the red-brown mantle on the crest of the ridge in autumn; and anyone wearing a uniform with signs on the shoulder is claiming to be acres of grassland held together by walls and bridges and railway lines, coming towards me, left hand outstretched right behind back; family, and staff, and you, and you of only yesterday, pine trees and inner suburban gardens swaying like tassels in the pre-storm wind: it all comes towards me, and one day we'll sink entirely each into the other . . .)

(It's all very well knowing what the tricks are supposed to be, but something else to survive the moment. Like stepping smartly aside into a platelayer's niche from which you may not be able to get out because you are a saintly statue. Or just going on, continuing for the present, striding on newly armed towards the green, ferny glimmer in the black distance, not at all sure whether the aggressive drunk passed to left or right of you or all round you like a waft of hot air or straight through the middle and not daring to look back . . .)

(From behind the earth looks very like Eurydice, on her way back to the pit.)

(The earth is scared stiff of us.)

And what if we endured earth's glory
outside the museum, outside the silence,
what if we bought something of the world
worth more than a Welcome doormat?
And what if we take the pain
as a factor of resistance and
continue, under the three protectors:
road, food, house.

>   The old man sits by the gas fire, cat
>   on knee, fastened to the portable TV.
>   All his knowledge is constantly averted
>   until there is hardly anything left
>   of him, and the masters of silence
>   talk unanswerably in a luminous blue mist
>   beamed at the soul's shell. So his dream
>   passes constantly, wider and wider
>   through him, and will, until there's
>   nothing left, poor ghost.

And what if we endure
the glory of this pain
anywhere, loudly,
dazzled by the actual world
articulating light
in my eyes.

>   Moving from day
>   to year his cap
>   is split, his heartspace
>   set in two.

YEAR CAP split heart
space set in
to partition

disfavour folded in
the air in the air

the city destroyed by jokes

For the breath is prompt but the limb infirm,
stay awake and keep talking, the breath
is ready but the carnival is insecure

And the shadows swirl and focus,
negative energy claims its form—
the abandoned mineshaft barking in the sky
into which this whole substance, not just
life, not just you and me, this whole physics
will one day be tipped, light and all.

The flesh is willing but the structure aches.

Our false language draws us towards the invert star
that sheds dark beams of disappointment across the towns
and those once as children so wholly engaged into life
by fear or joy walk heavily from door to door feeling
nothing but an inarticulate resentment that makes us
pull the blankets over our heads and snarl at each other
like trapped hounds / Colourless and formless ikons
of purposeless living, a talking photograph in the
living room to which there is no possible reply;
birth blood and battles for the sake of a tin hood
that does ninety and lasts a few years.

It is not respite, it is not safety or status.
July, tops of the ash branches already paling.
It is not your hand on my sleeve at the brink.
Valley hay fields full as the sea, a fold of smoke
hanging over the market town picked out by late
sunlight and every westward surface brightens for a minute
and surely the core of active wrong emanates from elsewhere,
not in our language at all or anybody else's—
not human and not world, not sense or nonsense,
a vague threat pulling from behind the galaxies,
outside the whole swelling sphere of time, of which
we are the skin, that we hold together.

We are beset by hypnotic clouds, dispersals of substance,
drawing us towards the void, artless existence
where all human constructs are interim, dragging
on the hollow spaces in our sensibilities,
results of ambition and restlessness which we thought
we had reserved for finer things, outshot
of the earth, at our return.

Nobody's writing The Phenomenology of Evil.
Stay awake and keep talking, fill the space
with substance, like an Irish brooch, draw out
the ribbon, fold and wind it into the enclosure,
which is the house, which means communication.
Draw it from the world's persistence. Tonight's
parcel post like a lion in the forest moves
to expectation, to continuity and response,
and what if perfectly solid men, men without
compassion, insurrect between us, toiling to
block the line with hollow gain—Nobody's writing
The Phenomenology of Evil and a moment's honesty
clears all the space we've got.

And nobody's writing the phenomenology of evil because
nobody wants to know. Each day the darkness shuts earlier
and behind the houses in old yards and neglected allotments
moths hover in clouds of seed under the arch of nettles
a warm fermenting vapour holds the night creatures in ecstasy
as by day the martins zoom over the stubble fields
in great ellipses darting between electricity wires
and again the earth is caught in full action, engaged against
its own inertia and which side could we possibly be on?
We continue not writing the phenomenology of evil because
we can't be bothered, because our brain cells decay too fast,
because we still have the space available of a more urgent
engagement with good, knowing that no one will ever write
the phenomenology of evil because, set in the outering vortex
we view it and there's no one there; it's a cloud of
husk-powder in the eye between two walls, a television screen,
there's not a soul to be seen.

Don't stop talking. Any error will unwind itself given the chance to stretch out, plus a good pull and a well-balanced back-tortion. But you must follow it through: don't just feed it new images all the time, follow strictly the tracks of your assurance down to its origin and counter—the recognition, the bit of truth that gave it a foothold on the earth in the first place.

And it occurred to me that language, spoken written or thought, unwinds a thread of perception out of one body into another (the "bodies" are compacted moments but the "bodies" are also real people) and we follow this thread across, parallel to our awareness of the present (held in abeyance, or displaced for the duration of the discourse), developing a tension between two concurrent senses of being (being here & now and being in transition). This tension forms, as its resolution, a third being, a third place, which is both leverage and resistance to the will-power which drives the whole process, and is formal in relation to the due return to actuality. What I call bodies, the origins and ends of language, might also be states, with forms, spheres spirals and cones, and the process could as well be a matter of feeding a screen, or indeed, writing a book. The book is a physical embodiment of the tension, the third mode of being; it encapsulates the transaction between direct and referred attention, it gives it borders, walls, and streets, until it is the image of the third city, the city which is neither here nor not-here. It is a city we can only pass through, because we are foreigners and cannot own or hire its spaces. It is a traveller's city, an Arabian stronghold packed with brigands and sultanas. We come here to market. Sometimes we are detained, sometimes for our own good, camped out on the maidan at the Kaid's (the author's) pleasure; but we shall never live there. We pass through this map to a new, newly gathered, entity, place or point, quite distinct from that to which the natural world would of its own accord drift, for better or worse.

Every human act genetically modifies the species, since it is only at that new point (of access and departure) that we gain our formal existence, and the moment is absolutely decisive in the future of the world and fate of its bearers.

What is the point of our being at all if we cannot advance by what we have made?

You get up, gather your coat from the wall, and go out, in the middle of my sentence, closing the door behind you. And that too, I'm afraid, is a linguistic act, bringing us to a new place. Like a gunshot.

Surviving fragments of the Solo Diatribe

… ignorance transformed by art into a damaging lie, the city destroyed by jokes …

… organs fixed: firmly and aggressively deviant, no entry, no risk, takes the skein of language and wraps it up, uses it for a, what, a belly dance? a spectacle? a sterile wrapper? Plunders the third city for reflections in symmetrical facets …

… self-dissemination, folding a tinted mirror at the world …

… without compassion, totally solid, stopping at nothing, they would fill us with their skins, the broadcasters …

… falsity made to bear the same structure as truth …

… in every way a copy of God.

and what but perseverance will carry us through this labyrinth of denial to the poles of day, where the black glass dissolves into the light and dark world: here, ordinary, personal, and lived?

Postcard: Please forgive
my silence and homily, say all
is forgotten and come back.

(Some reasons for the cancellation of the diatribe:)

Indeed there are other things too:
poems, or orders, which don't unwind
extend or delay anywhere but smite
in a flash to the centre of the mind:
You are to report to Divisional Office at once
for assessment / re-education / torment.
Delete as appropriate.
Your life is a poisonous waste.

Dead leaves in the emperor's garden,
flame and ash in one, floating
on the cold stone ponds.

DEEPER INto stone than any technology can reach
    is the stone in the heart / humanity partitioned
from itself by gut senses of uncertain belonging
    hinged on fear, the stone in the heart
on which a small bird, a finch, perches,
    tearing up the throat—
                      poems, and orders.
Deep clarity of pure dread, thin light cast off
    the crystal arc at dawn, floating in the streets
as the striped men arrive and knock on the door—
    whole quarters of the town change hands,
forced separation of families, lovers defeated and alone—
    chipped and scratched songs of sleepless nights
pulsing in the vein like trapped birds— whole lives
    donated to the structure, the facility.
So in our mannered fatigue we stifle the fleshly sparrow
    with relish and an iron hand grasps the heart
year after year, pitiless pursuit of reinforced advantage
    year after year drawing the human total down
into cavities of earth, dream, purposeless toil,
    concealed disappointment—
                      Dust of millions
grey sludge of bone powder run into the fields
    where it settles and weighs into the ground,
expressing pockets of deceptive honey, glassy edges,
    flowers blurred in ice, bright winged creatures that
flash past us in the tunnel, scoring the walls,
    smell of burning on the edge of the city—someone's
bright idea, deaths of millions and for what? by-product
    of an accelerated industrialization policy,
concerning nobody, vast unwritable acts of mass brutality
    always intended, by errors of substitution,
to do good, to bring relief.

Throw our guilt on the heap of clay stars
    and burnish love into the day.

AND THERE, at this very spot arrived at,
"under our noses" as Williams, and Orwell,
said, resides the difficulty—

unstructured and unstructuring particular
that doesn't want to be translated anywhere
and begins the answer about wrong and guilt,

that we call "anything" in our silence,
"nothing" in our fault. There are midges
in the air tonight, it's very close

and all the intermediary separations of the
distracting world devolve on this point
of attention, unsevered gate

that re-asserts itself into script, casually
through our bodies against all the pre-
human facilities of a controlled situation—

the midges prance in the clearing by the stream,
in the sunbeam, held there by the entire universe
and I am not reminded of anything

except the
        rotten old
                universe again.

Naturally it is adored from
near or far. Struck at a pitch of
valid energy the range is immaterial.

(End: underground impact course, 1-8

Seq.: the disaster opens to a new vein, 9-11 + ending)

HELD IN conative energy distance is acute
but the range is immaterial. And the impacted moment
settles daily into pitch as the absolute conditional
of living, the true the sonic diamond can you imagine
walking across a field without it? unaligned? future
flattened to a dead circuit of purposeless therefore
repetitive action? Nothing on earth is worth a glance
until our knowledge of it turns on the spindle
that cuts through memory and expectation and brings
the end of distance to bear on what's "under our
noses" indeed where we very carefully set it like
a gold fish in a green pond, scintilla, this
cocoon of light revolves on its axis as it holds
a human entirety in a state of transformation,
cells clustered in imaginal buds, that float freely across
our infrastructural (pain) webs towards the waking night,
there to unfold, carapace bedecked with insignia . . .

As anyone can see on the darkest day there are
cavities in substance, where the earth in its rush
to the day's completion tears itself apart and is
thrown against itself, rearing and falling—it seems
difficult to know how people, fixed or settled in their
various holes do steer the whole edifice by moral acts
towards its end, I mean quite possibly physically,
maintain the earth along the edge of time, every
bright leaf in sight taking the strain of galactic pull.
Housed in pockets of earth we play perceptive sense
onto resistant and laden masses at our focus,
prise open layers of rock, paper, fat, disrupt
all the sucroclastic harmonies that pull us towards
a rigid incompletion, by forcing the resolution. But listen
to the dead men mumbling and growling inside every pebble
of the vast shoreline, like a nearing bomber
or a disappointed crowd, listen to the unearthly noise . . .

And the saint on his tiny island in the bay
like a doctor in his surgery, islanded off
from the unhealing world and blasted out
of self regard by pressure of work—love
like this meets constantly the resistance of
matter directly as a gardener where every shrub
is won from nothing into the ancestral shield,
and the stones rise to the hand.

Sudden turn of winter in late April—
aubrietia in flower
under pillows of snow!

*

A usual day, taken up with mending.
We run through the list of jobs
and go to bed.

Only to face the entire circus.
Sleep is engaged to prospect into the hill
and does it—by the book, in straight lines,
dictionary and log tables to hand, using
a compass marked in two ellipses
and The Easy Method Surewin Pools Guide.
And sometimes gains and sometimes doesn't
but being freed, in the moment, from will,
always retrieves what is in fact there.

Organic energy tends towards regularity
and the end of that dream is law, the final
symmetry, the victory of flesh over stone.
For stone resists order and pushes down into
chaos and sameness. Flesh clears a space, a small
travelling theatre at the heart of substance which
as it goes on its way leaves a track, an engravure,
a furrow across the strata of occluded time,
traded for air and filled in with ink.
And dreams and laws with their musts and mustn'ts
in the end only delineate what is—
sentences of the Book of Reasons,
spoken by an ancient child
who crawled out of a hole in the ground.

Unable to sustain love we succumb to the strata
or tear out the jewelled ring at the centre and turn
the earth back towards us in the act of signature.

And we shall too, meet the night sky's lording
in what we bear, in every knot we wear.

THE CITY's surface and perimeter swollen
with lights, command of feeling as extended
and productive biological need, 5 police cars
and an ambulance, the slightest immediate
kindly act and the very gaucheness to say it.

The catalogues of favour slowly accumulate
in right acts of any scale, etymologies and
histories of musical instruments, whether in
rage or cheer we burn through the night of thought
until the flags descend on us.

All the work is directed to this grace
whereby in a moment's turn as in a year's
bulletin we are rehumoured, and cast
resentment adrift like a fishing line
in the earth's blackness behind our home

Oh lightly as if not bothered, to justify
being this forward transaction between soil & sky
that sharpens its claws on the city walls
and laughs at the tortuous blinds of earth,
knows them to a T and adores the green patina.

Than as the candle burns lower the spoils
of chaos are set in a wicker basket and brought
to market, bearing his fatherly self for smelting,
and courage is care, care is purpose, the weight
of earth falls off.

In the dreamshaft it was faster: door in
the whole, ore-body, world-image sighted
as a warehouse of the self from which
we feed us a supply-line into time;
but that copious garden (flesh and ash
crystallized in the night) is a globe
of perception under great tension that
at a touch flies open, bearing such
strength and focus towards us at speed,
faster than bone can ever withstand.

Deep well in hilltop garden as if
we could be lowered away and never
have to be bothered with love again,
but cultivate boredom in a national park,
barbed wire and binoculars, to the last day.
Look out of the window: the grass is hard
and quivers in the rainwind.
The hilltop garden is death's own plot
where we search for our ancient child in
the vorticist angles of our immediate trade
and its histories—

> *Oh if you will trade me for constancy I*
> *will seal the compact with my whole*
> *expression, my figure etched in the*
> *die my life sunk in the eye leaving*
> *nothing behind, not a trace. If I were then*
> *given fully might I be complete, un-*
> *merged or hard bound enough at least to be*
> *a spoken fact before the skullchild of our love.*

The substance, tensed and struck, flies at us—
we are cut, but can enfold the flint
in our cloth, can bear the news.

FLESH WITH
stands and stands
with
to the world's end.

Do you suppose you have any enduring structure,
anything worth offering and keeping save
the enduring imagination bearing on particulars
as loving care? Your life is an empty waste.

> The royal gardens fell ages ago—
> stone rings sunk into the ground, leaf debris
> and moss carpets over the paving flags—
> it is the world departing, folding in on itself—
> the trees spread at ease and collapse: of
> twelve birches, seven remain and a dove bone,
> thin as wire, leans under the turf.
> No spirit, no presence, no memory. Anything
> seems to be saying nothing, and all this
> material, stone, fibre, with no one to hold it,
> rots, swirls, and tumbles into hell.

But flesh is bound
to the meeting place
of earth and space
by the point of efflorescence
between the eyes

and tries
death's employ.

Adonaïs

The second pain is the loss of pain,
the shrinkage, and survival

Waiting for time like a long Sunday School procession
to meet its end—

Hospice inmates, retainers, industrial archaeologists,
busy up to the last minute

Plotting and preparing a past
for which it is long too late,

Death as the future tense of courage.
Awakened from working out life,

You brave entry
to what you are—

Crystallised blood on the lens,
windscreen wipers too slow for the rainstorm,

Big floppy leaves swept over tombstones,
and the tall grass swaying.

The Mission catches up with the Music
and we're home.

And the miners all dead, not party to any of this,
striding in vast tunnels under the earth
to and from the workface, singing
> *Con los minerales vine*
> *Con les minerales voy*

Pockets stuffed with burning jewels, trapped
in crystal, inhabitants of the deep translucent world
that is only the world we can see, cast before us, cast
outside us, for our advancement.

Sparks of flesh scattered on the earth,
flowers, that speculate, and call and call
till there is no rest to be had, the tower flats
buzzing and flashing through the night beside the river,

Procession of tail-lights on the motorway arm,
tunnel of orange glow, sweeping past the spangled
power stations and depots, clouds of steam lit inter-
mittently from below, brief flowers on a tumulus.

We are worn to a point in the clarified dark,
flesh smoke always in our nostrils and before
our eyes sharpening the distance towards the end,
the island home and true response—

For in spite of everything we are together,
every single one of us, dead and alive,
and something won't let us forget it, this
endless hammering inside matter.

The outside also matters.

Full moon, limestone ridge
a grey bank against the night sky,

Aura in the trees and round
the corners of the house, not a

Match struck. The mouse
squeaks in the grass,

The cat sleeps, dreaming
tomorrow into question.

The mines—they all ended
in a silent lake.

LINES ON THE LIVER

Der smit uz Oberlande
warf sinen hamer in mine schoz
und wohrte siben heiligkeit

The smith from foreign lands
struck his hammer into my chest
and wrought seven blessings

(Quoted by Novalis)

(a)

It seems to me now that any person or place we ever might suppose of ourselves will always be an excuse for being later than we are. To verge on, yearn for, or enter into truth supposes a distance which is not where we live, for very truth means that we are already there. The truthful distance which occupies our lives gains its language from within, as we range through from diurnal bodily pacts out to the stellar hazards of speculation, with always the same faculty of thought engagement that exposes love over the whole; and surely any wish apart from that continuous presence breaks it, and wrenches the mind into another journey towards itself. It must be elliptical, and can never arrive, if separation from the quester's own being is the motivation and stay of the journey, and defence from the world's inquests. And in that self-perpetuating self-seeking the human image finally eradicates itself, and occupies only the gap in the torque, the emptiness before the mirror (the mirror shows a beautiful garden or a child who duly responds to us or any other receding prize) and is indeed the nothing masked by writing.

But what about the journey which the unmirrored and unmirroring self constantly undertakes in its participation in lived reality: acts of love, queuing for milk, patient inquiry into the sublime, doesn't that also have its necessary script? and isn't the felt hollowness of living which writing seeks to answer something else, in that case, than a projection of the self's incompletion, a mere vacancy? What about that breath of fresh air when the self no longer sucks back its substance from alterity but betakes itself into its materials as a ready whole? doesn't the self then claim its entirety on the spot in offering itself right out? doesn't it become nonsense then to talk about the "wholeness" or not of something which is its own field of engagement with the world anyway? isn't the lack which drives us into work then something from a distance, if not distance itself? The cross of good will and difficulty realises the construct in all its detail: theatre of desire which bounds the singular space of the person as of a city. And he who freely chooses sets himself on the inner edge of knowledge, and drawing his life onto his shoulders, refusing to act as anything which doesn't completely coincide with itself, at once sets deformation and absence outside and visible, and stands alone before the sphinx which is the world asking back the disowned question about the failure of love. I mean why does all the perceptual space passing through us have to come out in twisted shreds of meaning or be ruled and chopped into bars and stored in jealous caves? The world itself is not like that, but extensive at any price in the terms of its constitution; and we eat without paying and commit cruelty by proxy as if we have no proper right to be here—what's the matter with us? The quest remains, not to find yourself but precisely to lose yourself into the interrogation, which as it persists in staying within your experience is that much stronger in its resistance to premature disclosure and resolution, than the selfhood coyly evading its own capture in public hedges, but is thereby disclosed and resolved in a far greater reward—the furtherance of realizable good. (There are those who will tell you, in the cloak of loveliness, that virtue is an event of the selfhood, and oh if that were possible we wouldn't need to lift a finger, we'd live for ever coiled in the dream winding backwards from the instant of good intention.) Then she gathers the past up at the hem who sets into such a venture, only the possibility of which is actually chosen, and arched against the blast is indeed the sign she makes, by which it is to be known that time is complete, and no objective will replace death.

(b)

I thought this in the process of moving house: not far, some twelve miles, eastward over England's central ridge, where it ends here in a terminal boss, a dome of ore-bearing shell-residue, a white capsule of sedimentary patience twelve miles across, patinated thin green and powered from underneath, lately christened for the tourist brochure The White Peak. This pendant pearl hovers above the magno-industrial parks and wastelands of a different centrality: the Midlands: flaky shale, coal mines, ironstone, potters' clay, executive dinners, that extends to east and west of the limestone, while to the north millstone grit marks complete northern refusal and reaches down to clasp the sides of the gem. A national park has quarried the King's Field down to school tarmac, but this is completely ignored. The princely townships of the plains are elsewhere, and a sense is taken of outlying stations, and a gathering ground.

Moving east, then, and setting up house well up an eastern valley-side, just off the limestone, facing west, as I had previously been just off the limestone to the west, facing east. What is behind me is then in front of me and I walk backwards into the future, a blind sense of desire which is normal to reading and thought, and having it tabulated here I take it up into the work, the figure of my spine, the S, the written creature that I send out into the dawn, eyes shaded against star-blast, tapping the ground—this is my guide.

This move, freely chosen, has me arriving here and climbing to my window seat on a diameter between two arcs: a diagonal tension across the land. I swivel my chair between west and north, and in front of me, in front of everything I say, always, is that pastoral dome stuffed with regal imminence tier on tier. It underlies my vision like a table-top mappemunde or a chest of drawers stuffed with prize money, the past halting itself at a plateau surface marked "Gently Dip, but Not Too Deep ..." Ring, clock-face, axle, compass: it is complete, and it suspends vision in stone libraries of forgotten voices fluttering against the skin, shells or kisses spinning like tops in the calcium night. Anyone could last for ever in that luminescent offer of gain, following a vein further and further into the ground, fixed on a wire of discourse whatever the consequences. But the Professor of History paces the eastern highlands behind me looking for his lost child and further away on all sides is a dull rumble from the offices of time, trouble up at t'mills. The intaglio demands a living body to wear it; the moment arches to contain.

My glance westward lifts, over the hills, and comes up against something else: another band, another lexicon, another development, stretching up through the Midlands to Liverpool and the Lancashire coalfields via Stoke. It's behind me too, following the clay and coal up to Leeds and striking across the Pennines to rejoin itself. It is a motorway community where the same replica barstool sprouts from one end of the land to the other and housing-space looks like something merely tolerated by commerce. A linear labyrinth of sameness, grimly dedicated to its own furtherance in controlled energy, boxes and tubes. It advocates soul-loss, narrowing purpose and discountenance and hides its servility to fossil fuels behind a contempt for grace. I occupy an interval in this thing, a temporary fork that closes above me, an eye, with the M62 stretched across it. I sit by the stream.

For over a century people have felt threatened by this growth as if unable to breathe openly, in or out of it. But it is difficult to resent the line of semis creeping up the hillside when the hill is as blatantly artificial as the homes, which is what they seem to be and who knows what may be given birth in them? What we've done is actually all we've got: the hill is formed and clad in our knowledge whether it's a volcanic plug or a slagheap in disguise. This whole encrustation of the world is a band which is fully lived, every scar and flake is a human result, and from where I sit it looks like precisely the result of that marine fossil energy in suspension which has men mining in their sleep, so much the result of centuries of human accruement, society dreaming itself into astronomy. Hundreds of miles of warehouses are the outcast from a tunneling into the hill of dreams which has no centre, so you can never arrive, and work and will become ends in themselves, for nothing.

But there is no self more industrially exploited and scraped hollow than that which views the great plains on the other side of the earth or time void of humanity and breathes a sigh of relief, as if it might be possible to act at last, on the edge of the grave. For this pressure is also a gravity and in its tense compaction this industrial displacement of settlement bears the possibility of a song sufficiently clasped in temporal ugliness not to lure us into the negation of all endeavour, whirlpools of aesthetic solipsism. I wanted to prove that the usurped space is also in the heart from the start, under threat, waiting or begging to be colonized, so that the regret must be a guilt. The circular hilltop garden at the ends of my fingers (the space being-written, always redolent with the sharpness of death) must have (there must be) a gateway into this archive of fear, where the hand opens to validate at large the coin embedded in the palm. The creating faculty (flower and completion of the whitestone dream) would then come within sight of the dark labyrinth and propose not a toleration nor an absorption but a trade, maintaining the distance of communication, and in that light the black stone breaks into crystals from within. But to submerge, to condescend, to inhabit urban boredom in its own terms would (to me with my shelves of ancient men chuckling drunk by the lakeside) be as meaningless a piece of self-stifling as you could think of, the sacrifice of the poet and labourer into the Great War and for what? The necessity (the men by the lakeside hear the word, giggle and nod) is for access to the great war that lies over all of the western world with coastal resorts as its Christmas truce, a war relayed from event to situation, in which the wastage was never greater. (It's all very well for the lakeside men, we only know them by satellite transmission and the edge is filtered out, the rhyme-scheme, the grinding work over generations; figures of ultimate reward, we get them by fake TV as surrogate parents, "round the corner".) And it is a war in which the enemy is yourself (how simpler it would be to have a simple parental enemy) contesting the right to be. As a member of this proud state I push it with my foot out of morbid curiosity. Sometimes when I switch on the news I feel like a migrating cuckoo coughing through Flanders.

But it's here anyway, again and again it is here without any previous notification and the heart inconveniently falls apart in the night. It is my own stomach I prod in the grass. And again the hand opens in social patience—it is demanded: the north wind comes tearing down the white cliff face laden with grit and smoke, a past which will not be gathered up free of guilt, and thought of the heart is also a persecution.

The primitive class-based tension across England North/West to South/East is a fake, a hat trick of northern comedians. It is not a tension of supply and demand, or raw materials and product, not since metal completed its circuit across the final human gap and the mines closed. Then anything comes from anywhere. Demand was fed back to supply long ago and the highland zone persists, on the motel screens, as little more than a packaging on urban squalor. There is some pull still between production and the vast mechanisms of safeguard, supervision and pictorial comfort, which we seemingly need in order to boil in egg, but this has no geography and both parties serve the same master: the nourishing and progression of the speed-web centres through which the dominant fuel can use us. This tension surely snaps the moment any participant looks up and wants to know what he or she is working *for*, and the whole of politics disappears down a hole: you are working to accelerate the decay of nature. The left hand smoothes the ground while the right hand waves a flag; the only reason they can't get on together is that their total work does nothing for anybody.

I wanted to add as clumsily as possible that the opposite of generosity seems to be built into this makeshift structure as its motivator (advantage), deceit as its linguistic vehicle. It becomes increasingly difficult to view the self or soul as something quite distinct from this edifice of lies, a purity soiled by its ingress—"language contaminated by commerce" but without commerce we die. The pressure of expectancy from the world of importance on anyone's performance is a howling constancy that everyone feels and the untruth deployed in maintaining the pretence of conflict is not normally willful, but rather hysteric and hypnotic. I would sooner believe that the uncertainties of intimate experience are themselves at the source of the fear which commerce uses and which the media spread everywhere. Then it can be recognized, since no one escapes it.

The only tension that finally matters is between this futility and its opposite, as experienced in states of hope. This true tension remains cardinal to a different geography, wherever there is space liberated for application and thought. So it is not going to be realised through the half-knowledges that entertain the visitor, but only in the mint vocabulary whereby anyone has access to reality lived as an immediacy, meaning the particulars are no longer in conflict with distance, but become solid objects as the arena in which they stand increases by a dimension. No one could actually "want" to be poked awake in this way from suspension in the present; a blast of ice-cold indifference down the telescope makes us start and we want to know with some urgency what the reward is to be, for we haven't got all that long to go. We also hate it, but have to acknowledge the gentler and more persistent demand of the totality which also reaches us down the inky telescope or across the white sheets or wherever the completion of the moment finds us. And this horizontal crosses with that vertical and there we are in the middle: sitting up and asking what time it is. Across the house, the land, the workshop, the mind, this diagonal pull persists, between what we can do and how it can use us.

If my niche is brought to the fulcrum of these forces where it is my life and nothing else that signifies it, then there is hope of raising a leverage or personal balance onto natural inertia, energy so much fuller when it is spliced into care. It can only be a personal act, for we play and are strung on these tensions in a constant engagement with the momenthood of our own humanity, totally distinct, and from this action documentation and magic are similarly infantile distractions. The scale of international discourse is so slight that the self shrinks and demeans itself to think of such a thing, and global market squabbles seem like faint echoes of personal acts long forgotten and superseded in the real world. It seems that a state or nation is something which acting as a person can only act at the person's meanest and most insincere. And maybe so it is if that is its function: to be our collective grasping and cheating for subsistence, our fear for survival. Isn't the hypocrisy of its claim to a function for good (so that it expands) the very point at which it causes vast and unthinkable harm? Isn't the wicked cheat of empire the reason why our comforts and benefits will in the long run fall apart leaving us at each other's mercy as public moral structures are again set aside in order to support business in crisis? I doubt if it has ever been any different.

Which is to say we are always stuck with this thing which is evil because it is never bad enough. I don't think in that case you can mend it. It's like a mass migration: you can't opt out and what you have to do is ride it—not cowboy style to glory but survive within or alongside it in order to stay where you are. There's no avoiding this literal involvement in public movement, there is no "quiet life". There is a pensioned-off condition of surplus time lag which it is an indignity to entertain, or there's the television lake village, sheer drudgery and categorical inequality in a pocket of pictorial solipsism, inhabiting only the wrapping of culture. No—we engage with the entire present or with nothing. Far from subverting or breaking the conditionals we receive as temporal tensions, the task is to raise them, to maximal balance. The tiredness, the administration, hell-bent on debasing humanity before its own facility, drags us across the world into alienated nonentity as soon as we risk ourselves into its function, i.e., project human fullness of soul into the hard, crumbling, ugly and disordered outer surface of the anthill of the state, and the lost souls who think they control it. We seem to accede to this political reduction in submitting to the choice of a career or detesting the government, but then we take the long road home. We grasp the fulcrum, and the luxuries of denouncing wrong give place to the duties of tracing harm back to its causes. And this movement, this progress that we move with, is only humanity's struggle to meet the demands of the inorganic world seeking to deploy us to its own ends. To attempt to retire from this civilizing confrontation can only mean a re-engagement with materials already superseded, the tools for which have been melted down. Marching into the abandoned mine out of "interest" and watching the ceiling crack open. The music deep inside the nest is the rumble of time brought to a gamut.

Every venture we make has to be returned from, every brilliance dimmed, back to the stupid hordes plodding over the empty tablelands in search of somewhere to stop. Back to the self, back to the price of tea. Very old people often have a way of making this return quietly and unto themselves, sometimes in spite of themselves, and others may force it with yells to the same finality. I mean people can be loyal to their ways wherever they are without damaging difference, for the map is of a wholeness too strong to be distributed.

As I actually arrive here I turn my back on the forces raging across the land, and probably derive resentment and envy from them in the most casual and irrelevant performances, and am the more pursued the more I am swept wide at the splendour of the spread, the sun emblazoning the horizon before withdrawing it from sale. To bring this to consciousness is only to say what I already know, to rescue it from the sociological is only to return it to an actual society inhabited from within. It becomes moral from the particulars outwards—where else could we learn the dangers of our own acts? Harm at a distance, tea workers of Sri Lanka in our 3 o'clock trap: it is already too late, and no sample sacrifices or megaphonic expiations will do anything but damage our own language. Our acts are *already* at a distance because what we inhabit is the world and what we do is done in it, and to it, all of it. That part of it within our scope is then all the more the enclosed garden, the working arena, the king's field and all its demands. We sup the bitter-sweet cup of our limitation and put the long-term question, seeking the acts and knowledges which will enhance perception itself, up to its node of healing.

To arrive and stay is to accept anyone's position in the line of the unwilled tension, at a balance. "Balance" may be an easy suppressive word, a tool against the slightest trace of living energy, the sense of single necessity that drives love, but perhaps that is a refusal to see balance at all until it is rusted into position. An active balance is in constant peril which is the peril of our lives verging on entombment in the world. Any option is a pretence: northern fæcal machismo or arty gossamer poses, each concealing the other. In the meanest version of experience there is always a counter-valency, and the effort is, as I said, to raise the balance rather than tip it. And whatever ancient works may, by their petricolous distances, persuade us otherwise, I can't see this as anything but a sequence of personally lived acts, taking the form of an answering quest. The questing movement and the stasis of leverage and balance cohabit finely, in fact this paradox is one of our best tricks. By this we might be able to equal the duplicity of fate, the way our acts come back to us as puns and transfix us in their terms however much we shift—the mysterious disguises and metaphorical transformations of human result, its automatism. By the duplicity of script we acknowledge and rise to the mechanics of fate, hoping to maintain good (not necessarily present good) within submission to justice.

We follow our own lights. The only common directive is the highest precept. I sit here facing the labyrinth of pre-waste at its Northwest corner as the site of personal histories abandoned, concerning no one else. I am challenged by the foci of harm beyond and behind, the concealment of good within. I don't ask for this obsession but having got it there is a chance of leverage. Stationed here, I open a channel of question and answer towards a point of attention in time, along which various futures come rolling back to me. By tracking this tide onto a new present I stake out a new past in the hope of preserving what virtue there might be to survive the absolutes of revenge.

What I do is, get to the window and look west, further and further west into and through the mist of past possibilities, through these blanket terms, ever narrowing down for points of memory set in the occasion like a carbuncle, that can never change. Taking very few images in the trust that this gradual closure (attenuation) of the past not only widens the present but also points the future (behind me) to its single lode, to eliminate the veer and swing of possibility, to be the better future that follows a completion. On the assumption too that only what does reach the heart will make any difference.

To the west, beyond Stoke, are Welsh hills and the sea, and eastward behind me stretches a simple and wide monotony to the coast, perhaps the most blessed condition of all land: unexciting and open. But the past I dwell in is not so distant, and the distance that worries me is not so extensive. West and East stay with me as I move around like a left and a right, while also beyond me and fixed. It is not a problem of extent but of accuracy, and the only true spatial index to that is the night sky. About which I am ignorant, and all I can ever salvage from such dizzy attentions is that up there there are fixed points, which only move with the whole, each as fixed as, and no more than, the whole. And out of so much space only these points mean anything at all; everything else is gathered onto the dark side of the moon and deliberately forgotten as unthinkable horror. And the other thing that emerges is that those points are constituted, and I think this has always been known, by stories as by telescopes. Stars, molecules, and moments held in memory: they are all constituted, and they all have histories. They all open into new landscapes under perceptual pressure. We don't reach a single end.

I can ponder and plot, but like everyone else in this society I feel the star map as something uncomfortably marginal. I look at it now and then and try to feel threatened but the challenge doesn't come, and I suppose that in a permissive context it won't. The heavenly bodies pin us onto the present with a force that passes through us into the earth's track, we know that—star laser straight into the brain where the strangers are. Coming down from immensity, bearing on the present from the total, determined to make us the node of its unbearable tune, as a perfection that destroys. Under tyranny the stars are solid and their beams, dead straight, transfix questioners into instant statues. The sky map, its points unopened, is the banner of every human fixity, and all that cold beauty brought down to earth can only mean fear and cruelty. Here in this west we occupy a kind of mess in which the same kind of thing happens, more or less through carelessness, as in avowedly authoritarian states, wobbling between the permissive and the repressive as the newspaper wind blows, but the same forces operate. The attempt to lurch sideways out of the fate-trap by sheer ineptitude relies on kindly errors which can't be trusted. The pressure is still on—we don't feel it or see it, but it is there. Surely the star snares shoot down the sky in the cold fall of light as they always have, surely they aim between the eyes. We meet the distant light and cross it with horizontal spread, or set it against its anti-point, or whatever linguistic resource is to hand. But it is here that we do it, with what confronts us, within our lives. There is a mineshaft in the garden. I can see it from the window.

And on the opposite hillside the quarries begin, ripping out the landscape for road-dust, for oily money is in a rush between banks. Staked here on a suspended earth-shift I scan the western mess for what survives from it as it settles into earth. In the first movement the reaches of harm come faintly, and the Celtic hills and the counters of Fortesland alike transmit faint and impotent moans: self colonisation, forges of nothing, time ground to a rubber band; fragmentation, vacation; resentment. All that becomes at best a gloss on the sphinx, a lamination of former joys, a loss which means nothing and for which I am responsible as I perpetuate it in my regret. There is also a false pastoral (which like all ways of writing is a way of living) which inhabits this gloss and attempts to mask the boredom in short-circuited dreamwork, leafy parabolas, ontological egotism—a reductive clarity that conceals the steps and claw-marks on the surface of language. It has caused an enormous increase in rural land-prices during my lifetime. It tells me in my own image that I can pass out of blame into a special-self, a suspension, reflecting the formless beauty that is already-there. Magic poetry. It is not true. All that alienation has to become specifically mine before it can even be spoken—my lies, my harmings, my concealments and their fruit on the ground, my twists of meaning. Tracing the event back to its source and forward to its result you have to own it. A bringing to a point, which can never be diverted to a generality: I, unfortunately, am the point. But then the guide is not totally blind, just wincing with dazzlement and shame, just groping in a wind of stone-dust, flapping at the accusations, just fully awake and wide eyed but only responsive to actual truth like a point of light in the clouded, earthen distances. It was us who clouded the distances, and narrowed the light.

It is easy to talk of getting or bringing to a point, like admission to regeneration at a door. The self becomes the point in the hope of returning the light to its wholeness, where it is no longer an object at a distance (lamp in window on far hillside, promise, star's reflection in flooded mineshaft) but "that in which we see". The self sharpened to a point advances to meet the star-like question wanting to scatter it, answer it, reclothing space in day. That also means bringing the self to a vulnerability which drives a wedge into experience as it opens a hole in the person, for the question to reach the centre. And my resistance will be my transparency and the tunnel through my chest will be my solidity. There comes then to be another self, blunted into indolence by the act of confrontation but resting on equal terms with the active soul. We no longer expect our divided selves, however many there may be, to stay in "harmony" like some barbershop ensemble through this process where one face is the other-side of the other, the black and white of some strange cone-shaped object and aperture. Mouth and throat as horizon wedges. Be content that they do subserve the heart, and deploy it into time.

The future does not just become the past after all: it is changed to it at a specific point, and in poetry we propose the "heart", as the only human point likely to be able to meet the blast emerging from the world's pin-hole. The heart is of course the metaphor or written sign for the purposive whole (in-one, at one time), offered out because it is thereby the strongest point we have, because its sensitivity is acute because it doesn't hesitate, because it resides in thought. Each bolt of reality chimes through me provided the quality of response will open these layers of fat to the instrument within, and kindly close them behind. Perception reaches out for glad tidings but has to take what comes and break it through the frame, to ring through the person (gathered up to that point) to an unknown future. Which is to say, that such arrivals solve nothing, answer no problems, assure no one's future, adjust no one's past. Yet, in our ignorance, all that is to come depends on our reply, every second.

The stew of pronouns in this section (we, you, I, he/she) shows my nervousness at seeming to hope that a few domestic poems can be central to such salvations and destructions, in what must looks like a theory of election. For there is a further sense that to refuse this exposure, to refuse to meet the truth which is the term of your existence is only to conceal the fact that you cannot refuse, and you do meet it, whatever you do, with no alternatives. For instance, as you cling instead to the comforts of earth you lose everything; the message comes zooming over the horizon in the end whether you invite it or not; you come to a point; you die. This has been pointed out often enough ...

And eventually, after quite enough of this cross-fire to and from the world and its representatives beyond the horizon ... I tilt downwards and scan the valley below and the town that lives there, which seems a greater distance, more difficult to see, than either geological chaos or industrial entombment. If you study the town you find it is a duple thing, living its own being now and living from elsewhere in another time. At night its lights cluster on a chosen shelf of the far valley-side under the quarry waste-heaps, and string out severally up the hills. There is time at sunset, or at dawn if I were ever awake, to know the one whole sentence of its two faces, a precise transcendence of its two truths. In the point of difference, the trading-point, the coin between desire and repletion, in the hinge of day and night lies the unique language between two translations, when the lamps shining in adequate daylight take on the force of stars piercing the blue and multifarious mantle, and seem to project the potent strength of all the souls that live there, and wait their reward. And the daylight is at such times close to horizontal across it all, direct or filtered, so that the sun's fixing weight, its necessity, is cued onto the very distance we know as home, and we are firm in its tide as persisting lanterns by the strength of our wish. And so we secure a very special position which is perfectly ordinary. This overlap has us shining in our works as only solitude can, in among the multiplicity we are no longer threatened by. But that is because that compacted state, the little place all spread out below and within knowledge as the aggregate of home, is hated and feared as well as it is loved. Out there, thrust in the narrow and brief alluvium between slices of moon rock, the created home is sheltered and sheltering, but it is also the place where we cannot postpone or quarter our rivalry for souldom and its cannibalism. That is, to enter it, and call it here: Then as a knowledge of the self it becomes fully alive and distinct, and the engagement is on: sparks off the head-axe, knifework in the narrowing eye, competition, investment, and all the noble duties of affection. This is all home within its own reward, as the theatre no longer of desire but of love, the "whole" because it is so much more than anyone could want.

My response to this double door is a preparation, a turning to the wind, that I would register, and hope to carry through into act the very light glanced off the quandary and the innocent persistence that reaches next day anyway. I set my stupidity against the town's and all this purposive self-centering breaks into a fiction of appearance, and a satire of luminescence. The town makes nonsense of time by its own clock. It actually eats into the hillside in a sea of roofs, but its hunger also comes justly back on it in huge undertows. It is exactly opposite me across the fault. I am lucky to be able to witness these transactions, and have to act quickly, for the tabs are already set on it, for further development.

(c)

If it is true I am here. But where? For although I mimic some symbolic ritual of renewal with "It seems to me now . . ." and claim myself in the open, classic East to wish to furnish truth as firmly as I suppose I inhabit it, this hypothesis does not in fact help me in any way to be my own exactitude. I cannot keep on arriving here, where I have already lived for nearly a year: I am sick of seeing things for the first time. Sooner or later I must simply be here. Then I would be free to write myself into anonymity. Then a story could begin.

But first the written orb has to be freed from the world. For the more it is "now" and "here" the more it is "there" and to look further is of course to look closer than ever. The more the writing emanates from a totally inhabited (person-shaped) space, the more it is liberated from obligations of representation towards that particular, which appears (in full) if it appears at all, caught in the completion of the text. Who'd want to be a ring-stone proclaiming its own setting, anyway? But I don't know at all the answers that fix such a distinction and settle the wide contradictions that rage about the furnace. I don't know where the guilt of withdrawal gives into the prayer of furtherance; I don't know where the furtherance of happiness finds itself in the open clarities of pain, and is bound. I only iterate that the whole ragbag has to be fetched "here", so that my personal space, which is of course normally "anywhere", becomes so engaged in the transfer that it can only possibly be at the one point it is at, without wrecking the joys of fortuity. Elsewhere is then distinct, there are no alternatives, and there is no direction for the writing other than its own, written, destination, which is no more than the perfected and logical firmness of the links it proposes. To be nowhere else is an augmentation of the angle obtaining onto the world, by the elimination of spread. Then you are fixed in the presence, veritably driven in, and the world stands still at last waiting for your answer and is a thing of its own, in which we are included, to which none of our affective terms necessarily apply. Every preposition begins to take on the sharpness of resignation, knowing that the final or total offer can only be refused; the very width of love returns it as a possession from the stone in which it is embedded.

We know this at the edge of the person, which is where writing, among other things, takes place. This edge is furbished to a seemingly inhuman sheen as it extends into script, but the resulting compaction makes possible an entity which as it is so completely itself can begin to act helpfully, undisturbed by the incomplete and unlimited denizens of seduction, the broken edge to the public image of humanity. Then surely the central disclaimer holds us together: what on earth do you think you can act *with* but who you are? And that instrumentality is being-here, and to exist here in that sense is then itself the result of the exercise of love.

In suchlike considerations poetry comes into being and continues to exist (cooling) in its own right in such a way as to corrode the self-absorption which prevents people from picking up old ladies who have fallen over when they know perfectly well that they would rest better if they did.

That is to say, to further the good act, which is known by its result and by its fidelity to its own moment. Possibly poetry can set up the fiction of inhabiting the moment sufficiently to delineate the good result of its completion. The old lady says thank you kindly and potters on, grumbling about the price of margarine and the lack of discipline in schools.

(d/i)

There is a single point where the pen touches the paper, of which writing is the extension, which is the mark of the person. So much writing is no more than that (so much of my writing is no more than that) and scared of the white space behind it knows only what is in front of it, does nothing but arrive (a continual zooming-in, perhaps never actually getting there). And since that flattering self-welcoming (in gain or loss) can only intend a meaning which is never fully present (this is rather like showing photographs of your self in some remote and desirable setting in case you're not all here, or so that you needn't be) the reader can only read herself in it (can only read what she already knows) because there is no whole or sited self for the reader to engage with, no mind to encounter, no resistance to her own self-welcoming into meaning (whether she "agrees" or not, or just recognizes her imago flattened into sympathetic spread). This is to dominate the reader, playing tricks with the mirror, inviting her to a determined subjective space. It conceals the fact that she is already in one.

The point of writing is not pure and it has to move. The point is a space (conceptual and metaphorical since any actual point is metaphysical) it is a marred space. It is scarred, smeared, and faulted like a limestone dome once subject to lead mining, teeth-marks on the shoulder and flank of the hill, like a pearl which has passed through centuries of trade, warfare, and domestic unpleasantness, like the full moon inscribed with all our foolishness and error. The circular garden is the site of a constant fight or coition, which only ends at the peristalith of a hilltop tumulus. So the constituted point has to move, through the years of seasons and meanings, leaving its trace, remaining intact, becoming whatever colour it enters but not forsaking its identity. Intact through its changes because it is the fixed mark of the person it bears, and, in the solitudes of thought, his only, cold, open, eastwards, home. If such a home—the durance of the edge of a personal space distanced into a sign—is not trusted from within, how can change ever be renewal? Such intimacy is a hard, and far, remand that releases affection to its boundless exactitude.

(d/ii)

There is a single point where the pen touches the paper, which is, as it moves into its fate, the mark of the whole person. The "whole person" is a fiction dependent on an actuality, the movement of the authentic signature under trust. Reported presence need surely be no more than that, and anything that represents an author adequately crammed into a corner of that imperceptible dot. The "whole" person is then the person in extended time where he or she can be known only by in and as his or her work.

But I seem to return again and again to this act as a kinema of my own daily doings, with all the risks of coy glimpses, domestic preludes, sentiment shifting slyly towards aggression or displays of seeming integrity with no second opinion. I think it is necessary. The moving planet of the soul passes through medial opposition towards a resolute polarity, and surely the delineation of good in that course (the completing of that course) depends, at least sometimes, on a singularity that can't be taken for granted in favour of largeness. Surely the ground of the act, intimacy, requires constant renewal from the centre in favour of largesse; a constant testing of habit and manner against result in living. It could be an anchorage or land-mark in polar apposition to fixed points of high purpose in the night tumulus above us. There are ways of guaranteeing vast scale on the instant: the point of singularity is stretched out to a hieroglyphic cartouche which slots into a pre-existing conceptual width beyond anyone's actual sphere of experience: social metaphysics! Well, I admire any attempt on History and only fear that in my present state of contraction anything vaster than a goldfinch means turning aside from the heart, and the bird in the hand will pine for seed.

Meanwhile, this rectangular machine, rattling through the night, this bone-box, crashes a fully formed stigma onto the skin at every stroke: the standard letter. On what model? Who licenses these chunks of meaning? The sign is at once a shield and a majority verdict removed from the beauties of any particular human visage as it reels through time. I insist that the heartscript is cursive, bearing difference at every point and unwinding its messages like a sledge-track in the snow—errant, and subject to the contours, but aligned. This stamping machine seems to reduce the act to a package deal, public from the start. I never use anything else; indeed I no longer possess an ink pen. Every word fights against its publication for access to the heart, as indeed it should. And the forward point is maintained in its own metaphor zipping here and there across the keyboard, as it was at the end of the nib. Metaphor defeats technology, but philosophy defeats metaphor.

(e)

And yet I remain suspended in front of the question. I move in, I install. I drive the world and its absences out of the house with a few practised fences: bookshelves, records, hangings. I climb to my window and station. I know the vein opposite, by its warmth and disruption: signs of life just under the horizon and further insecurities on the radio. I wedge myself into the ledge and insist on staying put, trusting that the more firmly my personal time-space contracts towards its (chambered) centre, the more fully will perception disclose the world's secrets, open as they lie on the surface of event. If I *seek* that disclosure I am back in the van again, in transit: nowhere. It is not itself a purpose. It must be a conditional of my being, a kind of birthright, the very script of my species. It inhabits the bright and dark fields of result.

We are constantly drawn out of this made space by insecurities and shady percepts, so that we become our own objective. Pairing becomes a mirror exercise and a whole "culture" is developed on the fear that needs constantly to be assured that if all it believes in is its own advantage, well that is all right, and important, and sexed. I WILL NOT STEP OUTSIDE. For sitting at home quietly at work on the tracks of love is the Bible of Hell to that fabricated world of lies we are led to believe we inhabit (by image-proxy, no one has ever actually been there), instructed by the defence of defence. It is the book to break the fixed, cloudy, faces of all the spokespersons of nothing, who would have us out there to the ends of our days stoking the furnaces of the smoke industry.

But this home shouldn't be mistaken for the actual refuge I am permitted to call mine in this world, where as soon as I set foot in the door I start owing. The home I speak of is real, and physical, and mutual, and there's a funny smell in the bathroom again, but as the site of work it is not subject to the temporal conditions of an uncaring administration. Oh, I pay my concern politely: "I hope your civilization will be better soon". I go to work. I take a walk in the abandoned quarries or a quick off-season excursion to Paris, but I don't budge. And to refuse the glass of that seeming exterior forms a different seeking, to explore the sepulchral anterooms of the heart for the world's engravings. My participation in the deception, as instructed on the screen, is supposedly provisional to the day when there is no longer any spare part of me available but I need it all gathered into the truth I posit by existing. And the punishment for this duplicity is my own obscurity and failure. Gaining the food where it lurks I at least retain the right to disclaim advantage. And it is in fact marvellous the way people all over the place hold this life unto them and run it into heaven without tax or insurance or anything but a simple number on the door. It is an elaborate script merely to notice this, and another to delineate it—the furtherance of joy, which I'm sure finds its authenticity also in the disarming validity of the expiring moan or wince of shame. And while I know that the home of writing (the third city) is set far apart from our earthly settlements and exposed to the biting and soundless air because of this, I still can't know the details of the force which finally coheres these aching distances, which can only be here on the spot.

The lines on the window are thick with this question in the conditional modes, the yearning again, the fall into possibility. Poetry may here move much more slowly than the gnomic prose of the self-lecturer with his prefatory sightings after the event; but that delay is necessary if poetry is to meet the world's resistance as a whole, at every point. The world demands its own future, through us but beyond us, every blade of grass a transaction to be thrashed out to the end for the privilege of knowing it. Muse Divine, aid us to win an acorn from the clash of spheres, defend us from fossil energy, the gravitation of distance into loss. May we keep us aligned to the final receptor, may we wrest one future from the doleful stroke: everywhere-present-now. We can make instruments to combat the arrest of good will against fear of fragmentation and spread (which is not the true difficulty), by setting the fullness of the immediate into the total as an intimacy. The world then rages all around, but we begin to hold our ground, our cælestial anchorage. And it is from us after all, that the energy proceeds whose devastations to left and right we grimly discount—industrial wastelands and national parks, twin capitals of another false polarity across the world ever ready to sacrifice us into nonentity for a shred of pride. For in vacating and dispersing the continuous human agency that we are, we lay it wide open to the usury of our own acts and end up a mere vehicle for the world's cycles of degeneration. Poetry or something steers us down the centre, powered from within, into the vale where the township lies, occasionally exploding but most of the time (and most of the time belongs to most of the people) lying there unhurriedly improvising its own fate. I like to think I encourage it, sitting here pointing west day after day, turning round at every meal.

LINES ON THE LIVER

Moving eastward under symmetry towards no,
not yet home, not till I get there the west
pales, the sky behind me a crimson slush, a dream
of statement slowly falling into bond

But crammed with people and brokenness, my solo
is concerted, I feel the tab on my collar, the
spine touch, and radial, you're always there.

I stick an ex libris
over a library stamp.
I walk the dark room.

All that happened
and where's the poem of it?
—there in your surface speaking
your body writing your soul

Tall
and never still
like the autumn grass

We could happen to
a Lycian double music
conjugates my throat weft.

for Stephen

Your mother left you in care
Maybe she didn't care
Who now is to care
for and about you—

That you manage,
and have to bear
these dreadful puns

And cruel rhyme
since they
drive their cares.

Something intervenes—it's
clearly not our nature
to desert. I set up
the new shelves from Remploy,
placing the closer demands
at eye level, & somewhat faded
or accidental emissions
close to the floor and ceiling.

There is no one but you in this stanza,
sitting in a chair at the window.

The first of three
challenges:
To the Office

Why do you fetch me through
abandoned industrial premises
broken skylight

For what joy is there in stinting
and what can ever keep us
but what we turn out

Unsettled, furnace bracket,
Northwest gritwind I
catch on the brow,
terminant under decline.

Why do you lead me through
derelict factories,
25W Pearl

O tackle these impressed spirits
on the shoulder, the vertical I
speak of is no one's vantage,
adjusts no one's past—

People are ruined,
live in holes in the ground
at the mind's bequest.

That's not life—
that's a bloody paste factory!

Why do you call me through
gaping circles
with every trapping comfort
of love except fire

While the proximate and named
you all the time keeps me to a greater
issue, globe in globe or arm in arm,
continuation to mind of those murderous arcs.

Six hours into night and I'm nearly what?
20/40-what? and what persists—
space, stars, and the singing.

What do the bookshelves care if we
reckon a loss, what does the town
conclude? And further on is what else—

Space, stars, and the track
the rider makes in the sand
singing difficulties and durations
into holes, is that us?

                                    Letters, and boxes,
                                    with or without
                                    messages

The old postman died
The new postman tried

We occupy the vacancy like a small boat
on a green lake of postal orders, a Sabbath craft
pushing obstinately towards Wednesday week

Couldn't you have tried a bit harder? Just when I thought I felt
    like getting something a bit important in the letter box
    or at least something demanding immediate action like a
    book by John Riley or a letter from Tuscaloosa there was
    this splat and there on the floor was a beige existence a
    demand an acknowledgement or something sent by an
    anonymous plinthed limb in decorative projection which
    didn't even have the courage to hurt me and the little
    boat grounds on a bank of ice-cream and nobody dies
    any more, there is no more horror or violence or danger,
    behind the little foggy window of the window envelope
    there is nothing at all, to get upset about.

The postmen are weeping
the premen are sleeping
the stars acreeping I
wouldn't wait.

Window piece

One of the little squares is out—a previous occupant
stretched polythene over the space and sometimes at night
a moth flies into it, sudden thud

cf. I think I'm "getting somewhere"
sudden thud
you're behind me.

The membrane holds. Ktd4Xe6! black
moves. And now there's a dead moth
under the cover of ten years' diggings,
a streak of grease and money dust.

Here out of my writing
your fingertips glow in the darkness
you climb into the valley

And I know my life can never be translated
out of this miserable little hole
full of novels and possibilities—
the very sides of it cut my hands.

On the hard rocks of the heart vale
our sight ends. The magpie moth
lays her eggs in the wound.

Spend an evening like cream cheese—
the organs are poor guests
to pain and starscript

Waste an evening on limestone—
neither work nor company,
just resentment's luncheon.

Too late perception unbinds its numbers
and head contacts metal fire direct
splashing blades on passing flames
ah yes I'm blamed, too true too.

I couldn't say any thing

the Day as proved

what, what for Heaven

sake the Day has proved.

The post is a tale told to get me up
up and out in the eyebright fields

But breakfast is closer without a news
and subtle streaks enunciate return

We should reharbour forgetting against
history, and live the trade.

To R. Crump, somewhere

Such a commotion in the grass!
Can't you see all the little mortifacts
running around, can't you see
John Cowper Powys
bending over a bracken pit
and striding off again
to the nearest stationers.

Now is the future to any past, *upon us*!

Can't you hear the music of the garden of the earth
running screaming from the nearest box office?

From Liverpool to Leeds
a bonfire thrown on a motorway

For a white smile, for a coated neck
we have razed dignity from our homes

Your excellent teeth and the light down
on the back of your neck I shall remember
as long as I live. We rivet our time
on happy needs but then overseek— oh it's not
ours to question, we surely are to answer,
surely, are, a shower of sparks, to enunciate.

It's awful—there are owls and townships in the night
and I'm trembling because some Sales Manager
said "Now look here . . ." on the phone.

No resolution is anticipated.
The owl, swooping over, looks ahead,
the town sucks vision down its lamps,
I quarry into night a day's end.

Perhaps it's just that after so much
rooting in humanity
we need something to dry our hands on.

There are ways of knowing
if it is true

If it is true
there are ways

There are paths across the glassy crust
that change every hour
"... and the flesh severed wholly
from fear or calculation"

To arrive, to stay,
breathless in two.

Two complaints: 1

I'm dragged off into the world world
the one with wax ears and no genitive
no duty, no justice, no true cost— I'm
caved in! When all I need is a cave to
sit in and concentrate, a serenity, my office
drags me through the counties like car stock.
There are ways back, strategies, and
exercises. I follow the ground, misreading

1419
The Flash between the Crevices of Cash.

Second complaint

I'm offset, I inhabit the line
between you

Riven with storm centres and my
boots leak, they are ridiculous!

Speech also is a burden, one day to
conclude and pass like a car in the night

On this heavily scarred dome when the
bright ring is full of flesh

In the silence of our love every pronoun
calls down the sky, our constitution.

Dust rattles down the stairwell
and is ground in

The wind hisses between roof slates
we are smudged with the honour
of being so close

Smile too at the sky's blade
as it strokes the heartboard
edge to edge

Where it stops at your
truth, raise it.

> First of three
> disclaimers, which
> break the rules

I'm not this totally solid man you posit,
I don't take his praise—love
is at least specific and my great ambition
is to specify this bewilderment which
moves through me like knotted string
though at other times it is more like
being pressed onto the diagonal wires
of a harp-shaped entrance. What exactly is
like this is, for my part of it, no more than
sitting here at this nightly settlement, witness
to the changes of light where that includes
or indeed amounts to love which in its turn
involves and under certain pressures
amounts to, the necessity
of knowing harm
                    specifically
so that there are lines, of high tension,
indicating a pulling presence in the world
solid and clear, product of you and I, to which
there needs to be a response. The light falls
rapidly and the time switch achieves its
notch—the lamps come on. The response chimes
all over the horizon.

For this, I'd have thought, for the chime
of the response, a certain hollowness
is needed. But a hollowness
which contains. Contains what, I wonder.
Heart, chambered seed, stop
rattling around when I'm trying to think.

I'm not this filled person you idealise.
If we drank it, the Grail, would it act
like warm milk on instant potato and some
soul substance swell up and fill us to the
inner surface of the skin, so as then to
coincide with the form of the person and
we'd act as nothing but that, whatever
it is, poetry, love, truth, heart? Is this
why we court selfishly the light and heat
turned on us, the reflexive beam, because
we long to nurture some kernel destined to
replace us from within which we do or
don't call death? But what of the space, the empty
and tough vacuities which the heart needs
in order to function, and what is that function
anyway but a stopgap device between our ends?
Aren't we more likely to overflow with loving energy
when what expands within us is an activated silence,
a bolt of alien space no part of us at all, as when
we recognize the world's constant nul response to our
hearty well-meaning thrusts and shame and anger
blow down a straw into our sealed centre
the very breath of patience. Then we are
brought into parity in a flash of linear contact,
stone to heartstone down the throat, and
more than ever in years of good time
we slowly lever ourselves into balance
with the whole, the abomination.

And in the very early morning
the first lorries go out again.

I'm not this remarkable character you entertain—
my throat is cloudy, my eye oppressed,
and in English my You is diverse.

I don't anyway see how any person
could hope to attain to a greater degree
of sufficiency compaction and cleverness
than a brown berry fallen in the grass;
look at it sitting there with its maps
and its charts and its migratory tables:
it settles its fate before it starts
to a plain contingency—
it waits to be eaten. And the grey
wiry grass of the uplands
bends over its taut brow.

I hope for the heart chambers and ventricles
of the lungs not to become that one-off man,
speed-winner, screen-eye, professor of grasp.
But leave him alone and let him be—
let him be filled who will not fill,
let him be clever and let him be sure,
frozen to the pebbles, nothing
but suction,
              pseudophallic man,
nothing but suction.

Ruined castle, ruined poet,
ruined husband

See how the earth twists and cracks
round to meet your fate,
your first chance.

Lesson, translated

At one time
I, frightened, ignorant, hardly living,
covering up my eyes with images,
claimed to guide the dying and the dead.

I, sheltered poet,
set aside, hardly suffering,
dared to trace paths in the abyss.

Now, lamp blown out,
hand more errant and trembling,
I start again slowly in the draught.

Philippe Jaccottet,
Leçons, 1966

             The anecdote, the fall

Among so much natural beauty to slip
on the snow and fall flat on your back,
on the wooded hillside the trees draped
in crystal and floss, there to note
your feet disappearing from under you
and thud. And you sit up, and you stay there
while everyone fusses around, knowing
that this is as far as you're going.

"Do you feel like getting up yet, Mrs?"
"No, I don't."

The valleys spread out below, all the cakes
and candles they've hung around you for weeks
and at a certain point, thud, and that's it,
you've had enough, poor soul.

If our humiliating experiences
could be relied upon to make us humble
before something worth it,
something actually "up" like
a human soul or the length of days,
we'd live on sledges
and confuse the stars.

Three apostrophes
to the town—
two then one

It's a town of cake-eaters,
the houses shunted on top of each other
and sown out under the cliff— everyone
wants a slice, and gets it,
spitting still fertile seed onto coal.

I love the cubist streets,
reared up and casting the light about,
our work, our walls, all our
power given to the moonrocks
and coming back so dangerous and firm.

It's a town of nutcrackers,
solid, big chested
workers with
circular faces
faced into the cliff face
where the threat lies
level-sliced,
infertile,
mollusc revenge
on the people.

					Coming or
					going

One thing
always only

pen on table / gathered evening

one thing wished and
one thing worth it

seedfract / matchless / gathering light

heartbeknown.

PROCESSIONAL AND MASQUE

THE REPLIES

There is a particularly bleak part of North Staffordshire near Leek where you can stand on the very edge of the Pennines and watch the illuminated or brick crusted industrial flatlands run away before you towards North Wales or Liverpool. It is the edge of a plateau of high moors of heather bilberry and moor-grass, where denudation and burnt-out atmosphere have changed scrubland into miles and miles of growth failure. So where "wheat, rye, oats, barley and beans" were growing in 1385, with pasturage for sheep and cattle, only the sheep survive. This high edge overlooks the Upper Churnet Valley and The Roaches, with Stoke-on-Trent in the first distance to south-west. An unclassified road runs along it. The moorlands behind, about four miles wide, are part of the gritstone clasp on three sides of the Derbyshire limestone dome. To the east they slope down to the green and white hills at Warslow and Ecton, and high land prices start again.

It is an area of empty disregard, brown grey and purple against the faint, scattered, hidden greens. The convexity of uplands repels the human transmissive-receptive organism and they are felt as the back of something. The only buildings within miles are occasional stone farms tucked into protective folds of the moors, some operative some not, and one former drovers' inn now relying on car custom in the evenings. An army training camp under the edge sometimes sends bands of tender youths in khaki to roam these wastes in single file, with trucks, jeeps, and flares at night.

And yet by the side of this road along the edge, at a junction where one road dives down the side towards Leek and the other follows the top onwards, on the west and edge-ward side of this road just where the ground begins to fall away, overlooking everything, the Post Office decided for some reason to install a public telephone box. It stands there alone in acres of moorgrass heather and peat groughs, precisely 1519 feet above sea level, exposed to the constant wind. Was it put there for the sake of the army, or the sheep farmers, or even weekend hikers? Who could actually have been conceived as needing it, walking or riding down the vast horizons clutching their few pence? Anyway it doesn't work now. The 'phone is completely dead and there is no light in it at night. When it had one, if it ever did, it would have been visible from miles away to the west.

I used to pass it quite often driving to and from Leek. Whenever the weather was bad John Dooley might be inside it—he used it as a shelter against blizzards and driving rain. John Dooley was virtually the only inhabitant of those wastelands: a shell-shocked derelict who appeared from nowhere after the war and settled there. His single occupation was to walk the moorland roads all the time. He was always somewhere up there; any time you drove over the top there was a good likelihood of passing him on the road, even after dark. He wasn't old, though often referred to as "old" as a dissociative habit; he was about 40 and big, with a large black beard over which his eyes crow-like regarded without comment the passing car. He had a habit of stopping at the approach of a vehicle and turning to look at the driver, the way people do in the more remote villages where visitors are scarce and people expect to know who's abroad. But he was never known to approach anyone, army or sportsman or stopped car, and I believe he found speech very difficult. He was strong: he plodded unfalteringly up the steepest hills and walked like a machine the ribbons of tarmac pasted on the moorsides, with the same dark overcoat in all weathers and a large sack over his shoulder, said to contain empty bottles, or by some accounts, old newspapers. He slept in a hollow he had scooped out under Warslow rubbish tip. What was his daily bread, or how he weathered the arctic Februaries, I've no idea.

His presence as the denizen of those wastes was nothing to do with the place. I mean I'm sure the only reason he settled there was that no one else had. An unguarded municipal dump in Birmingham would have done just as well. He was not interested in moors, landscapes, views, walking, seasons, highlands, wildness, any of it. Among all that wilderness his own milieu was entirely industrial: he never stepped off the tarmac and he slept among old cans a few feet from a steel skip. Spring up there was a slight and delicate operation which he may or may not have registered specifically or verbally, but he clearly had his own concerns, and was busy.

The only remaining question might be the state of that faculty of him once known as the "soul", and whether that had a language. And if it had, how humanly inhuman might it be in its demand. How it might speak only of the final pact between the person and its existence, and the final masquerade of truth overmastering silence in the total image of the individual. That it might be the very voice of the not-self.

For the other thing I remembered was one night in thin driving snow and some hill mist my headlights caught him in that telephone box, staring straight out, not at me, as I veered onto the top of the climb. The reversed pierrot mask: white brow and jowls on one of the small windowpanes, the rest, with the beard and the eyes, black. And I was past in a flash, but he had the receiver to his mouth and ear.

Blackshaw 289:

THE REPLIES

1. Walking east towards no more home
   Be careful what you think (feel, dream, etc.)
   It changes everything.

2. What we could is no doubt inclusive of what we never fancied.
   What happened is (like me) tall, and
   Never still. My trust warp hates it.

3. Out of care,
   I watch the lesser cars shoot past,
   Accusing no one.

4. I am totally unremployable.
   There is no one but me in this statement
   Of error.

5. Resentment is the terminal of our decline.
   I crack it on the edge
   With "Flowing River Song".

6. Speaking as a derelict factory I think
   My mind requests what my tongue lacks:
   Air! Space! Light! Fire!

7. What greater issue is there
   Than Man, tucked into the horizon
   And folded round a stone for luck. Fire!

8. Fzzz. Is there anyone there? Fzzz Fzzz.
   It is difficult enough, to love death living
   In a hole in all the rubbish at any age.

9. Someone breathed on the whole window.
   It's pitch outside and I'm not weeping.
   I itch with the ramifications of truth.

10. Every day the light climbs the earth trembling with
       veracity
    And passes on. And the knowing hand retains
    A speaking coin—your move.

11. If I stick my head out of this miserable little window
    The sky clatters over us preaching fidelity
    And at night a slowly declining suspension of fear.

12. My mother and my father, my children and my wife
    Lie elsewhere calling each to each it's called
    Counterpoint and I spent every last penny.

13. The day has proved
    Cold, with a thick mist
    In the late hours.

14. Officially I have forgotten history
    But am remembered by officers.
    Actually God howls in the sack.

15. This box is my office. There is
    No remission, no getting through without paying.
    I pay me till there's naught left and stride off again.

16. But we cannot begin to answer until the question is
    Through us. Like a little hooked noise: why
    Does love fall short, who do you think you are?

17. We also are the brutality that sets
    The questions and disposes.
    Nothing, no literature, helps. Now look here.

18. Separate from sky, separate from ground,
    I say humanity is perfect. I have
    Nothing to lose.

19. I have nothing to complain about. I know
    I am not to keep. I have been told. And suddenly
    The light reversed into a lake, underholding creation.

20. They said it was me.
    They said it was me.
    They said it was me.

21. In the morning I arch my back
    And prise my living between the spheres.
    We die from within, uncertainly.

22. I come nightly to my nightly settlement.
    I may be human but my heart is a dry pea
    That hurts a poor princess.

23. There are weak places and dead spots in everything we do.
    Don't worry about them. Don't let them fool you.
    And the lorries go out again on the roads of destruction.

24. What you are doing at this moment (how
    Ever) is called Living a Life.
    Not hoping to be, or other. Welcome.

25. There is space, and rain on the grass
    Where a small house once stood,
    No signs of ruin.

26. It is possible to start again so often you
    Never properly get going— writing a life
    And living a writing, of something else.

27. And there are nights with nothing but starlight
    On the steel rubbish bins. I am
    Confused about this, but cannot help admiring the aim.

28. My eyelids hauled up on the pasty nightscape
    My revenge on myself by time and air
    My halt in the scar in the scar.

29. Oh trust your one possession the only bird
    Worth keeping was Charlie Parker, you and I
    Never met a happier man in society.

30. Man in society, try to be more precise
    And also cut out the wist
    If you want to see heaven.

Notes

Remploy: a business manufacturing furniture, set up by the Labour government to retrain unemployed workers.

25W Pearl. A low power electric light bulb with misted glass would be described thus.

Ktd4Xe6 is a chess move.

The quotation "... and the flesh severed wholly ..." is from a story by Kay Boyle.

1419 is the title of a poem by Emily Dickinson.

Philippe Jaccottet: "Autrefois, moi l'effrayé ..." in *Poésie 1946–1967*. In a 1994 printing the seventh line has been changed from " j'osais tracer des routes dans le gouffre." to "aller tracer des routes jusque-là!"

Blackshaw 289 is the telephone number of the telephone box referred to in the preceding prose.

FOLLOWING THE VEIN

I–III

THE SPHERE descends into the cleft striking

sparks from the walls. The diameter

is fully sexual. →The miner

revolves his arms at the mineral face, the pick

curves over his head and in that wheel

are the child and the old man in that wheel

the male child and the old man opposite

each other on the rim their mutual weight

conveys impulse into momentum

alternating strokes of linear time.

At each stroke the old man falls forward

and the child mounts behind him, but the entire rim

grinds constantly against the shore, the sparks

shoot off, the child dives over his head

and marks in a flash the limit of his futurity.

The miner turns his wheel following the vein

deeper into substance, he accepts the challenge:

to rouse and threaten the conditional thick in armour,

professional authority declaring that love

is an event of the selfhood. This diameter

comprehends entire rift and city—the field

is tipped on its side folded in two and

petrified but the horizon remains

at completed distance, a life we can

only participate in, never be. It slopes away

beyond our cope and is subsumed in matter.

The line of farewell

                        is a pointed arch.

UNFOLD THE line and the triangle
springs forth, an apex structure dreaming
the rounded arch, dreaming us back
to earth. →As the miner bears into the face
the woman is more than at his side she is fixed
in the side of his knowledge and from that
copulation the ores are already melted the
metal runs glowing out of day's furnace
and the flames wing round him each
to each, birds of passage pulled through
his limbs. The flashing globe rolls
over the hills, circles the horizon,
aureole of the liveable space. From this
the fireworms shoot into the sky
perch on the masthead with their
beaks unfold the centre: his right
to be there, to be this work. The old
woman and the female child, the app-
ointed balancers, the sides of the road.
The female plane presenting uniform
pressure onto time, not stretched but

ranged, tenure on future drift, central traverse
across the city edges: hospitals on the right
battlefields on the left: patient wounding,
aggressive healing, fair death. We notice then
the centre of a sphere, some distance
before our eyes, which depends on our
work for equipoise. Deferred to that point,
the dark shroud is lessened
and pushed behind.

SO, WALKING down to the manifold the river
curves round to follow, dimly lit or
underground as it rains and if eternity
is in front infinity is behind, and white cliffs
to the sides beyond the meadow trees.
Topside of the ripple reflects daylight,
the negative is concave, the whole band
flows to the side and past us. This flux is
trusted or we are at a limit. Pythagoras
showed that matter cannot be reduced
to indivisible atoms, that the course
is by definition continuous remote to
remote otherwise minimalist reduct, we move
only forwards, we only say yes.
Or no as the case may be. Which is untrue.
And how could we anyway, with that solid
bolt up the spine, set to any process worth it?
Memory of the womb, memory of the
spermatozoon striking the egg, all the
unknown fractional lives across earth and time
participating in the self but here consolidated

in the channel, a unity entirely responsible: I.

Only the present then can be finite, only

the potential can cease to be, the reward as real

as the revenge. The first strike into possibility

remains intact through the web and the narrowness

of the divide and all the torques and all the guilt

is refined out of it, we are interested

in being complete, → and in tracing the metal thread

as it darts between mirrors and surges through

to the end of the connexion; which we

don't know and never shall know but

shall be having been able to have known

and that therefore it does exist.

Two Essays

A Note on Vein Forms

The principal and fundamental vein form is the "rake", a fissure in the limestone which normally surfaces and runs cross country any distance from a hundred yards to five miles or more, with a width if up to seven metres. Rakes generally trend east and west, either or both ends submerging. Their formation predates that of most landscape features and they run across hill and valley regardless. The rake is packed with minerals which were originally deposited in layers on its sides, and are now broken up and mixed with clay and broken rock. The greatest quantities are usually fluorspar, calcite and barytes, each dominant in a different zone. The lead ore (galena, crystalline lead sulphide) occurs as a low proportion of the vein content, in separate lumps, running through in ribs, or packed into cavities in the walls. Galena is a metallic substance, of bright silver lustre when freshly broken or exposed, tarnishing dull grey and crystallising in modified cubes and octahedra. In an average rake it occurs in quantities best described as "reasonable" but whole rakes or sections of them can be void of ore. A mass of ore is a "lode" and mining is a matter of "following the lode". Veins are "quick" (with ore) or "dead" (without ore), and a vein exhausted by mining is also called "dead", so that in this metaphor the process of mining is a combat aimed at killing the vein. Much of the traditional vocabulary of the trade, and mine-name etymology, represents the ore as a living substance or animal in this way.

No downward termination to a rake proper has ever been reached. But the fissure can close upwards, forming the rake "ceiling". All rakes would originally have closed upwards like this, but most now outcrop due to the weathering away of the limestone strata. The outcrop of a filled rake would be indistinguishable, to the untrained eye, from the rest of the land surface, but the old miner claimed to recognise a vein top by various symptoms of "heat" and reluctance of the vegetable cover. But in locating a vein the metal divining rod was the more normal and reliable form of prospection. Anyone who located a vein was entitled to start mining it, irrespective of surface land ownership, subject to a code of conditions and tolls, and following certain ritual observances.

The mining method into a rake is, in the first place, opencast along the rake top. The ore is then followed down, removing all the mineral content of the fissure in the process and leaving behind an open chasm, one or two of which remain. As the ore was followed deeper into the vein (breaking the rock by burning and later by blasting), it was found that the business of raising to the rake top quantities of commercially valueless material along with the ore was increasingly burdensome, and it became the custom to stack this material up behind the miner in previously cleared spaces, and above his head on timber platforms and supports wedged across the fissure. These practices came to form a kind of vertical labyrinthine structure which could be of great complexity in large rakes, with additional complications of irregularities in the rake structure itself and its extensions. The propped masses of unwanted minerals and pure rock ("deads") would become unstable as the timber decayed, but the constant formation of stalagmitic material from rainwater filtering through the strata tended to cement them.

Rakes were also mined by vertical shafts along or parallel to the fissure, from which vast cuttings ("stopes") were made sideways along the course of the vein, filling in behind and above with deads and again forming a vertical labyrinth, but one which does not open to daylight. In the available documentation of miners' lore, these huge, incommodious and dangerous structures are already established as the work of past generations of miners, universally referred to in the singular as "the old man". This ancestor figure was responsible for all the non-natural features of the mining environment, and thus for a lot of the difficulties and dangers of the occupation— a total conditioning governor, a figure of necessity. The name was transferred to old mine workings themselves, becoming the term for the entire condition of human intervention in a geological arena—it was all *because of* "the old man", but it also *was* "the old man".

The principal, first, or "founder" shaft of a mine was known as the mine's "eye", and the surface world returned to through this hole was the "day", whether it was dark or light at the time. The tiny circlet of sky peering down through the blackness to oversee the work of the mine was the old man's one eye, a contraction of the circle of the horizon to the span of a day's work. It is a simple, casual, but unrelenting vision of fate. In some of the poems of *Tracks and Mineshafts* this focus, the circle of plain with townships and routes across it transferred to a director at the back of the head—an ancestral scope narrowing through the person and out again to the future—is used as a figuration of the self at work in perception and creation. The mining environment is a world lost for the sake of world, but the image, coin or medallion, of the real, human, surface world, must always be there in the miner's pocket, his intake, or the world is lost because it cannot be returned to.

This working environment is a place of immense confusion, multiplicity, the marsh of random detail. In the mid-nineteenth century someone calculated that a miner in a big rake spent about one-third of his working day in the process of getting to and from the actual point at which he mined, the "workface". The workface is a scatter of tiny lights in the rock, a dim and broken illusion of distance reflected from the old man's eye as it pierces the miner's body. If it is the promise of forward gain it is also a jumble of dully gleaming memories trapped on a lunar surface, faint reminders and lost opportunities awaiting the blast of purpose. Miners were always very reluctant to work on rock which was "dead"—such work seems to have annoyed or bored them as against the value-engagement of operating directly in the channel between ore and day—so the minimal amount of clearance was done in order to gain access to the mineral body of the vein, leaving just as much room as was necessary in order to pass through barren rock: squeezes, crawls, tunnels about two feet square, and "coffin levels": longer tunnels carefully shaped to the dimensions of a small man, widest at the shoulders and narrowing down to the feet, a coffin extended into a corridor. Delay is read as obstruction and difficulty as against the agricultural images of delay as waiting and recurrence, where the different acts become equally meaningful in their sectors of the ring. Metal mining, which is the first mining, is here modern. Or the metal as coin and then displaced coin carries impatience into banking. But in the lead mining zone of Derbyshire, known as "The King's Field", there was a customary retraction from forward gain derived from agricultural imagery.

The mining continued in this progression, deeper and deeper, until forced to a halt. The water table was the lower limit of the workings, and it could be lowered artificially by various means to several hundred feet below the grass, a thousand or more in big rakes through high hills. The forwardness of mining is downwards, into the earth as if a falling deity had crashed through the earth's meniscus and had to be excavated out. It is itself a falling, and in its field could figure the ramifications of loving attention, as against the sentimental "width" of, say, space-travel.

A rake could sometimes be found to be "slickensided"—i.e., the walls fluted and polished by movement of the fissure sides and content against each other in geological time. If such a surface had a coating of galena it could be polished as bright as any mirror. At some places the stresses produced during such rock movements remained unrelieved in the vein, and when struck with a miner's pick the mineral body at that place would explode, ". . . like a fired Gunpowder, or a Blast in a Rock, so as great Lumps rise up and fly about along with a kind of *Terrae Motus* or Earthquake." (Short 1734). In one such explosion on record (Haycliffe Mine 1738) over 30 tons of rock were brought down by the blast. Miners were at times killed or injured. "I have seen a man, when he came out of the

Mine, only a few minutes after the explosion, who regardless of the danger, had pierced this substance, and was much hurt, and cut violently, as if stabbed about the neck and other places with a chisel, whence he was unable to return to the mine for two weeks." (Mawe 1802, Odin Mine). But often there was some kind of aural warning of an impending blast, variously described as a "creaking" or "a singing kind of noise" and also "like the ticking of a church clock", which gave the miner a chance to run clear. At some mines the miners were able to make use of this hazard— the miner instead of the usual piercing of the ore body made a series of small cuts with the point of his pick from top to bottom and then left the place for several hours. On his return he should find the vein-stuff ready mined: broken, collapsed, and lying on the floor ready to be picked up

The great rakes were the primary routes by which mineralising fluids reached the orefield, migrating upwards and westwards from the direction of the North Sea oilfields. The rake is thus a channel as well as a wall in the subsoil. It is an exception in the even spread of sedimentary strata. Limestone is a business of horizontal settling, layers of shell-dust, best understood in the images of sleep and suspension, whereas the intrusive minerals may be understood in images of dream and death. But it then becomes important that the rake is nothing like a volcanic vent, and there is no question of the challenge and valuation represented by metal being the fruit of an upsurge of "hot" emotions. The rake is integral to the limestone, though nobody understands its origins, and inhabits a much greater time-span than volcanic intervention. Its processes are extensive and strict. It is a clear set term, ruled across the landscape.

So the rake is not an intrusion or flaw in limestone but partakes of limestone's regularity and settlement. Whatever challenges and complications the worker faces, the rake still represents normal day-to-day continuation of work. The value of the metal is, in principle, initially set by the kind of quantity that a concern can expect to raise from a rake over a given period.

But the ore was spread beyond the rakes themselves, into branching fissures and cracks connecting to the rakes, bedding planes and water-worn cave systems. The ore was borne up from the depths in suspension or solution in thermal waters, most likely in the form of suspended particles attached to tiny air-bubbles in fast-moving water, and deposited along the sides of the routes. The continuation of this process, and/or redisposition in successive flows spread the ore further, into bye-ways and pockets. In these extensions the ore tended to be deposited in purer, unmixed substance, and in greater quantities.

There are several categories of these deposits, from small mineralised fissures and cracks ("scrins", "stringers") to wide horizontal deposits on the sites of underground lakes along bedding planes ("flats"), but they are all versions of the same thing: the minerals spreading into the available space. The most serious form is that called a "pipe", which can mean almost any ore-body of irregular shape apart from the rake, but basically pipes are old cave systems along bedding planes partly or wholly filled with minerals, or solution cavities likewise mineralised.

A pipe will always connect to the rake, but the outcrop to the vertical vein can often be obscure and indirect, and the pipe located only by following a thin thread of ore or other mineral (a "leader"). It is like the discovery, by skill or fortune, of a store of ore in the slow process of descending the vein, like the jar of ORANGE MARMALADE which Alice noticed on her way down the dreamshaft. Like a late nineteenth century investment trust in a great hurry, she missed it.

But a pipe is unknowable. It occasions great hope, for the ore is likely to be pure ("soft and kind") and can occur in any kind of quantity. But it is not usually an evenly disposed deposit; it bellies out and contracts along its course. A pipe can at any time contract to the size of a keyhole or swell out into a cavern full of minerals. The records talk of "boulders of ore embedded in soft clay"... "caverns lined with slabs of galena three or four feet long, the walls shining like mirrors"... "and at one place, one could stand on a floor of solid galena" (Stokes 1880).

A pipe will always come to an end before very long, after which the normal business of following the vein is likely to be a regression. One pipe can noticeably affect the price of lead in the national market, and to protect this price mines with rich pipes have been know to restrict their work to something like three months in the year. The whole nature of the mining concern can be transformed by one pipe, from a small or individual affair, for most early mines were one-man businesses following a minor vein for subsistence supply or less, to an underground emporium. Then it suddenly stops. Few mines were ever able to cope with this immense variance, and a rich pipe finished them off (I am inevitably reminded of the fatality rate among small poetry publishers caused by Arts Council grants). The economics of pipe working were never satisfactorily discovered in the centuries of mining, and only the large capitalised mining companies at the end of the history were able to come near to managing them, at the loss, of course, of the ability to cope satisfactorily with normality.

And the rake too, the constancy of mining, must have an end. Rake veins tend to dip in their length. The mining naturally begins at the upper (usually eastward) end, or somewhere in the upper middle, and gets deeper as it extends along the rake, sooner or later reaching its crisis where the rake roof meets the water table. The capacity to unwater mines increases technologically; the rakes continue to dip. The mines close.

But rakes also tend to decrease in ore with depth, except for pockets of redisposition. This could be because the ore particles in the mineralising fluids tended upwards (especially, of course, if attached to air bubbles). Ore was then deposited most abundantly just under the ceiling or cap which all rakes must originally have had. If the mineralising fluids had been liberated into the open air most of the mineral content would have been dispersed, and run straight back to the sea. In its arrival, then, from the bacterial obscurities of the North Sea, the ore was as it were held up to us, finding its greatest concentration and abundance precisely where it lay within reach "... as if it was the top Branch, and very Flower of the whole Growth" (Hooson 1747). Only subsequent disruptions of the primary process took the ore into difficult or impossible distances: displacement of sedimentary strata, folding, volcanic intervention, rainwater percolating through the hills. It is a providence in which we had no hand whatsoever, and indeed our very physical existence became possible by the same processes which halted the ore within our grasp. It is then all the more interesting the way the miner "gardens" the mine as its maintainer and protector as well as its exploiter. And the dark, persistent, penetrative work processes of the mine are intimate to the whole of our being, as much as the patient waiting and regular spasmodic outbursts of agriculture. The darkness, the refusal of width, struck me as very like all the creative processes in which love is specific, and the reward instant and permanent rather than promissory.

The natural progress of the ore seems to be cyclic in a very large span. Being brought up close to the surface of the highlands and set and crystallised there, the ore would eventually be eroded by weather and washed in suspension back to the sea, there to be deposited alongside shelly matter to form future limestone massifs, elsewhere in the world. Humanity's intervention in this process is a bridging or short cut, facilitating the speedier return of lead to the sea, reducing it to a purer form so that it dissolves and rusts easily, and placing it so that it comes into direct contact with water in the biosphere (lead water pipes, church roofs, coffins, bullets in the hearts of heroes . . .). The lead content of oil bypasses the whole mineralisation process as rain absorbs it from petrol fumes in the air. We are possibly not the only facilitating agent, for lead returned to the sea might depend upon absorption into the fleshy parts of coral and other sea creatures in order to be kept in association with calcium carbonate in conditions favourable to the eventual formation of a sulphide (viz. mineral enrichment of sea water in lagoons due to evaporation, plus oilfield hydrocarbons . . . etc.)

In the history of the industry the immense problem of depth working against water, the ore becoming unreachable, came to a head in the later nineteenth century, just as the value of lead started falling as it was being superseded in most domestic and architectural uses, so that the revenue could less and less support augmented technology. And the craft guilds of mining had decayed into industrial management units inapt to the disposition of the ore, demanding constantly augmenting productivity due to the terms of capitalisation (constant anxiety states) while the ore got less and less as it got further and further away. And all these endings gathered together amid choruses of pub and doorstep groans and blamings and whole communities wondering what the world was coming to, and talk of "decline", when all that was happening was that the metal and us had had enough of each other, and the socio-industrial structures were not versatile enough to move on. The discovery of a rich pipe would have seemed like a solution, but the factorisation of the mine had rushed the mining on down, right past the stratum at which pipes occurred, with its technological efficiency. They may well be still there.

But in another sense lead itself, as a metal, has its own built-in failure. The redundancy of lead was due to the forward vision opened up by metallurgy. The demands that the ore made on human processes by its down-spiralling disposition in the earth was a form of work unknown, to remove yourself so *far* from the living space, really, anticipating only a thread of subsistence. The only previous time people had gone this far from day was in the Palaeolithic, and there, it seems, voluntarily, for a self-sufficient purpose. The socio-economic results of metal passing through human culture set forward gain before agricultural recurrence. The old miner, the old man, may have maintained reference to the earth's preferred circularity by which any human process hangs on to beneficence, but that duty was easily neglected, the coin artfully debased. Metal is an unstable (and poisonous) substance, as the ore isn't. The metal is an incomplete thing, a lost lover, it seeks to reconstitute its ore, to rejoin its oxide or sulphide and hand in hand they'll run down to the shore. It will not stay. Any function we put it to is interim, any structure it supports is temporary. It is a fluid substance, always bending and drooping and melting, rusting and dissolving. It gets very tired, and wants to get back to its limestone quilt. This animal-like quality is in contrast to stone or even wood which at least stays as it is until it breaks or decays. Metal fosters impression and appearance, and clouds truth. The sculpture in metal is moulded rather than carved. The total vision of the stone ring becomes remote.

It is as if we were being used by the substance, as now by oil and uranium, whatever they want of us. But lead is not, as its ore, in any hurry whatsoever: it will wait for ever at the top of the vein for the rock to erode over it. It is we who set the substance into a rush and an uncertainty, by taking it out of its container and holding it up bright and exposed to the atmosphere. It could be a vast mistake, but so no doubt are all such ventures, seekings of death in life. There is no alternative, and we are best to charge into the whole process, rush the lead into the ocean in its melancholy chair, use its quicksilver fire and its serious weight for whatever good we can steer it through. All we can do with gold now, it seems, is bury it, as if we are frightened of the value we have set on it, as of its attraction, frightened of our own desire for that cool fiery glow in each other. We demolish entire Transylvanian valleys and evict their populations in order to get it, and then we bury it. We prevent gold from reaching the sea and we refuse to use it as either coin or ornament, as something *visible*. The whole mining process is a bringing to sight, and what is in sight is available and evident to everybody, but there are evidently bigger profits in secrecy.

And the mines gradually wind down, pack up and abandon, leaving a few scars and overgrown holes in the hillsides. Populations shift and transfer their labour to somewhere else. The rakes dip, and we translate that geological situation into the active verbs of our own events, the terms of our lives. We live under as well as on the earth's surface and follow the future down, and this must be the Promethean sacrifice— the loss of most or all of self, time, and history, into something than which we know there is more, and gladder.

But getting down to the real stories, where that deadening necessity crosses and interacts with something else, vertical thrust of the pure (constituted) moment, and carrying that crossed, enhanced, presence forward along our lives to echo the next arrow of fortune, and the next, and the next, till we build up a habitation, tracks and fences, a language, a hope, out of it all.

References

William Hooson, *The Miner's Dictionary*. Wrexham 1747

E. Manlove, *The Liberties and Customs of the Lead Mines within the Wapentake of Wirksworth*. (in verse) 1653

John Mawe, *The Minerology of Derbyshire*. London 1802

Peter Riley, 'Peak District Mine Names: a preliminary survey.' *Bulletin of the Peak District Mines Historical Society*, VI.5 1977.

Thomas Short, *Natural, experimental, and medicinal history of the mineral waters of Derbyshire, Lincolnshire, and Yorkshire*... London 1734

A.H. Stokes, 'Lead and Lead-Mining in Derbyshire'. In *Trans. Chesterfield & Derbys. Inst. Min. Civ. Mech. Engineering*, 1880–1882. Reprinted 1973 Peak District Mines Hist. Soc.

A. Strahan, 'On explosive slickensides'. *Geological Magazine* IV, 1887

W.W. Varvill, 'Secondary enrichment by natural flotation'. *Mine and Quarry Engineering* vol.27, 1962

Lead Mining in the Peak District. Edited by Trevor D. Ford and J.H. Rieuwerts. Second Edition, Bakewell and Littleover, 1975

Theses on Dream

> 'The war was a sleep, deep and animal, in which I was visited by images of an order new to me.'
> —Wyndham Lewis, *Rude Assignment*

The dream is the experience of retrograde time. From any point of time the dream looks backwards, and constructs a past, which is not a real past but a concoction made up from any available bits and pieces of the real past, or anything else that comes to hand. History, the construction of the real past, is the precise opposite of dream. The moment of waking is the moment of time from which the dream normally constructs itself as a retrospective narrative, but all through sleep the facts of bodily sensation are explained away by a whole series of dreams, of which we know nothing. The flesh can never stop dreaming.

The moment of waking is a change from one state to another, which the sleeping mind cannot face, and so some more-or-less preposterous explanation is fabricated, of the bodily sensations which re-assert themselves and push through sleep into waking. This is happening all the time in sleep, which is a constant struggle between sleeping and waking, but only at the final victory of waking (when sleep gets tired) is an explanatory narrative constructed such that we come to know about it, because we interrupt it, and it transgresses into waking perception, which retains its materials. Any moment during sleep has its own dream sphere which is full of the experience of momenthood which must remain unknown because it is outside time, and so is instantly and completely forgotten. The waking dream is something like a thread drawn out from a sphere of dream by the waking mind, or a grasping back for a piece of security out of sleep's vastness.

There is no sleep without dream, as there is no awakedness with it. Dream is incompatible with the linear time perception we call being-awake. But at the point of transition there is, it seems, a kind of overlap whereby the waking mind, seeking to know time again so as to resume its narrative function, reads the night's last dream as if it were a temporal sequence. Or the sleeping mind feeds this attenuation of the dream to the waking mind to ease the transition to a linear world. Or the waking dream is simply the collapse, and fragmentation, into time, of the dream sphere, whether that is one thing or many. Whichever account of the process we favour (and they are not mutually exclusive) it is evidently a necessary process, and must always take place, though not always positioned so as to be perceptible. The transition from sleep to waking is not direct or immediate; there is a gap, which requires a bridge.

Just as bodily awareness is a constant threat to sleep with its dreaming, so there must be a dream-like force which constantly threatens the awake state of consciousness, and constantly seeks to return it to the instant, spherical modes operative during sleep. We do not in fact ever fall asleep until we have voluntarily renounced forward thinking, by which I mean the mind's engagement with real time rather than anticipation or picturing the future, which is itself dream-like. It is our active, working awareness which the dream threatens and sometimes undermines, our realism.

It is in the nature of human perception constantly to multiply its possibilities and bifurcate its routes, so that the pressure of dream on reality can be understood in many different forms, from plain tiredness or day-dreaming, up through all the modes of practised perception in opposition to or manipulative of reality, to depictive skill. All these things disrupt or displace our day-to-day working engagement with linear time as it is lived. The very act of reading abstracts us into a progression which is already-there as a whole.

Dream in its widest sense is something which refers life away from its linear base, to an elsewhere which is conceived as a wholeness—indeed any sense of wholeness may engage this process. Obviously there are forces which bear on life in this way as necessary and beneficial agencies, which open the focus of linear perception towards actual wholeness, a whole life, the world—things we shall never know in reality but need to take into account. But there must also be forces inhabiting the same structure for contrary ends. So there are "dream" agencies dedicated, by lapse or purpose, to perverting our senses of reality, breaking our immediacies against programmes and secret agendas—the construction of a false present out of a broken past, the subjective assimilation of reality to a particular bent, personal or institutional, a torsion or fault in our whole perceptive mechanism which brings harm.

Think, for instance, of how the seducer's agenda (whether intellectual or physical), involves the construction of a false, surrogate reality, piecemeal, out of real and unreal pasts, and the agent opts to "believe" this construct, quite wilfully in certain instances, openly contradicting it at other times. Spheres which are incompatible are forced to cohabit as episodes. This invasion or conditioning of reality is a "dream" not only because it is fantasised, assumptive or subjective, but also because it is partial, and cannot reach its own conclusions in reality. The outcome, being subject to real conditions, will inevitably by different from what was projected, perhaps radically. It is a glimpse of an uninhabitable realm, and must necessarily be interrupted and abandoned, an untrue story drawn out of an unreal sphere, the wilful sacrifice of accuracy into a suspended conception metaphorically related to sleep, to be halted or cancelled or to run into death. But good will, the one thing whose virtue is assured, inhabits the same structure in modified and moderated terms, and the difference may be very delicate; perhaps there is not necessarily any difference other than the quality of the intent. A carefully weighed knowledge of possibility constructs a future scenario which, like the seducer's self-image, is a dream.

All the time we posit non-realities, futures instantly stuck together from pasts. How can you even open the fridge door without having a dream of dinner based on real and unreal pasts? Any focus on a sense or a purpose probably at once evokes its "dream". It then becomes a question of the faculty to prevision knowingly, realistically or honestly—that is, to bear the focus on *through* the dream, to condition the intent from experience. Then the dream would come under personal control, as something known for what it is, and as a reference to a sense of wholeness without which we cannot be expected to create or achieve anything worth knowing, we cannot work to a good end. That would be the contrary of the kind of wilful release of subjective distorting forces into the world, the invasion of truth by anticipation and intent (whether cynically or naïvely conceived) which pervade the fantasies of power, where personal and impersonal realities destroy each other, and thousands with them. Or almost anything on television.

The dream constructs a tableau, which the awakening mind, because of its inhering focus, can only recall as having been a series of events occurring to the self, helped by fragments of real memory incorporated into it. The dream takes place at the very point of waking, at once and as a whole, but is remembered as leading up to it. This unreal past is viewed in very much the way we view the real future – hypothetically, fragmentarily, conditionally. In both cases the time experience is projected not actual. Things are "pictured" rather than seen, and this image-positing process is surely also what happens in the decay of memory, when images in the process of being lost may be replaced with instantly fabricated substitutes, even reaching a point where the whole story is more-or-less completely forgotten and replaced with a simulacrum drawn from the whole sphere of the self, a dream—unless this process is resisted by a sense of allegiance to reality.

The complete dream, which we never know, builds up a theatre of the individual instant, like a tapestry, the appearance of an inhabitable space with its language; a world, but probably not a flat surface, rather something elliptical or spherical which encompasses the dreamer on all sides, some shell-like enfolding. Perhaps this is an image of sleep itself; perhaps this is non-time covering time. But we can only come to know it as a narrative-like condition without beginning or end—

the end is always interrupted by waking and the beginning too far away to be known. In this seeming narrative each event is unfolded out of the one which follows it—a cause posited from a consequence, an emotion from a sensation, a pure hypothesis of origins. Each occurrence, then, fathers a previous occurrence to explain it, thus creating each time the illusion of a new, older, point of time, which in its turn is explained or transcended by another new earlier event, and so the dream structure goes on receding further and further back from the one real moment of initiation. Analogy, association, echo, pun, and a thousand other tricks of the mind are the machinery of this construction. I think this receding series is probably always regretted in its furthest distances as a lost origin, or a lost understanding, like the isolating perspectives of de Chirico's early pictures of the edges of despair. Like the "cradles" which ethnic nationalists create out of superseded zones on the edge of or outside the nation. It is actually not a series but a unit, and its parts (the events, images and messages) are instantaneous: they all lie next to each other at one moment, and are indeed the mind's landscape or "content" as of that instant. The sequentiality, then, is the result of the scanning operations of the waking mind, always partial but to some extent haphazard, scanning what must be conceived as more like a space than an event. The dimly recalled or lost "earlier" parts of the dream must then be items which are further away from the point of waking (at which we pierce the dream and see into it), or parts to which there is a greater resistance. The quest to reach further points creates the illusion of time passing, viewed in retrospect. If the dream sometimes represents this as a forward quest from an arbitrary lost point towards a dreaded conclusion, this may be no more than the dream's typical duplicity.

For the dream reveals and conceals, but it is not truthful. The dream builds up its tableau from available items of memory (and possibly from elsewhere) while the mind is in a state of complete relaxation, so that no wilful acts of censorship can prevent the incorporation into the dream fabric of material suppressed in the day. This is where the dream is revealing, for building up this image-sphere on the instant it takes whatever is immediately to hand as its materials, with no reservations and no questions asked. It thus deploys what the mind as a whole actually dwells on, whatever the voice claims to the contrary elsewhere. But relaxation itself operates a form of censorship as it precludes difficulty and concentration. So in the dream there are evasions and concealments – crucial images or messages tend to be either hidden behind something else or thrust off the edges of the narrative (before it is remembered, after it has been interrupted). These are the lost "origins" of the melancholy dream: things we don't want to know, things we don't want to be bothered with, things we are entitled to forget.

These evasions, whether necessary or not, must be the work of the waking mind in its scanning procedures, and not of the sleeping mind, which certainly doesn't give a damn about what we do or don't "want". It seems as if the original and entire dream might hold some form of total of our experience in relation to that point of our lives at which it occurs. The waking (scanning) mind as it pierces the dream fabric at once orients itself so that what it refuses is furthest away (at the lost beginning) or behind us. Or, as the scan approaches some crucial point of the reverse narrative it diverts to the side, protecting the mind from the unwanted image by substituting another. The emotional experience of dreaming here may be that of crisis, perhaps *because of* the imaginative effort of substitution. And all the time in the timeless suspension of the original dream sphere this evaded, perhaps unbearable, thing was simply *there*, alongside all the rest, no better or worse, bearing no more or less weight than any other item in the dream's vocabulary, since the entire structure is without consequence. But what is this unbearable thing which we never come to know, and how do we know that what is unbearable is the hidden thing, and not the surrogate image? How do we know that our fear of it is not just the expenditure of mental energy needed to steer away from it? And how can we possibly identify it without risking rendering important and unbearable what may have been merely a diversionary spasm of a mind acting without responsibility. We define it, of course, for our comfort and to satisfy the demands of what we are.

The dream is revealing also because its evasions tend to be inefficient. The mind is faced with the task of viewing an entire past which is completely new, so it seeks out corners, tracks, bridges, walls to define a manageable sector, and from this map seeks to eliminate direct confrontation with disruptive factors by placing them to the side or far back in the past. But there is really no time to spare for the niceties of this arrangement. A plausible phenomenography has to be constructed *on the spot* and there is no time to check that the components fit. The dream is full of false joints and cracks by which the light of the whole sphere pierces the fabrication. And the factors concealed from us are "disruptive" perhaps only because they are concealed and would wreck the makeshift narrative if they were manifest.

And the dream-linkage, the loaded, oppressive, or absurd surrealism, is not evidence that the dream gives access to a pre-rational world of meaningful sensation which is how we "really" conduct our lives. We don't. The surrealism consists only of the blunders of strict rationalism in a terrible hurry. In the dream-narrative any kind of connection, anything that can be made to fit, will suffice, as long as some kind of narrative is cobbled together, however absurd or disturbing it may be, any kind of ramshackle hoarding to shield the self from the totality of the complete moment. It is indeed the very wholeness of the dream-fabric which the waking mind cannot bear and avoids at all costs by tracing out its one-eyed story on the patterned ground; with such inefficiency that mother's pained expression becomes a trap-door in the floor before you know where you are or can summons up the power to prevent it. All you can do then is fall into it, and wake up.

(None of this, by the way, is an argument against highly figurised, dream-image-laden, apocalyptic or even surrealistic writing, since such writing does not necessarily claim to reveal and prioritise concealed substrata of consciousness, and even when its authors claim that it does, they're probably wrong. When it works it may be the most powerful way there is of forming a surface language of connections and distances among entities of experience for a true notation of perception working at its most intensely moral pitch, which includes fidelity to the realities of echoic abandon. Where it fails is likely to be where it opts to function within a route or system, like a dream-narrative, which is something we cannot construct consciously without falsifying its entire nature; or the constricting programmes of official surrealism. Both of these imply that there is something more real than the real and that we glimpse it in denials of working constructs. A true figural poetry multiplies the real upon itself. The invasion of actual intellectual discourses by dream procedures, so popular now in the sleep of western academia, is of course an entirely different matter.)

If we could inhabit the moment we would be able to contemplate and dispose its contents so as to understand completely our motivations and the terms of our acts, and at last properly set them on a better course. This implies another time stratum in which we investigate the components of the stilled moment. This fictional time stratum might be related to the alterations of the time sense in art, work, and dream. Possibly art, or some art, sets up the fiction of the inhabited moment being scanned for the sake of the future. Not only might visual art set up an arrested moment at some optimum (formal) point of leverage onto the world, but also the operations of stress and elasticity in music and poetry, could at least disorientate the unremitting time-flux and project in the completion of the work the image of time crossed with something else. These acts would then be related seriously to dream. It will be a fiction of course rather than a confessional, because it is the working of its materials, not the expression of them, which multiplies the perceptual strata.

The dream itself inhabits the moment without art and without will, so that we are helpless in it. The dream's bounty is gravitational. It does array our living (some of it) before us like a book in which we could read for messages of consequence, but we have this display in the mode of falling – disjunct and arcane—and we are left with a kind of comic-strip waiting for its story to be written in, urgency in an unknown language, shorn of consequence, and often very obscure. It is precisely *dim* that rings true—

> Of the dim wisdom old and deep
> That God gives unto man in sleep.

For the dream is not itself the total moment, the authentic representation of all our being at one time, that is its source. Where it leads is where we are already led, it is where we incline to. There is a waking resistance to that pull which need not be false. We are easily led by the dream to a self-centrality where the world is read as reflection on the surface of the mind, we are led to a "depth" which is disregardful of alterity, even solipsistic, a depth claimed as a personal quality. This manifests itself particularly in the act of re-narrating the dream in language, where it will inevitably become confused with waking needs. Finally the real world (in whatever format we believe it exists) is pushed and bent into the enclosive, self-referential patterns of the dream (as in the story by Wyndham Lewis, *You Broke My Dream*). For the dream is the very simulacrum of the self, a person rendered as narrative, place and event. All consideration of it is self-contemplation until you ask of it the final question, as to what it *is*. To the dream the world is a closed shop with big lit windows. We are asked to relax into this (by delight as by fear) and possibly shed some delusions of impersonality in the process, as no doubt we should—the dream makes it clear enough when the need is urgent. But the demand of the dream extending out into the world is untrustworthy. "People of the world, relax"...into what? return to what? loosen and fall into what? There are parts of the world where there is really nowhere to return to at all. If we aren't aware of them, the dream will never mention them.

And another thing that dream will never tell us, is that strong emotion and good emotion are not the same thing.

It is strange how the intensities of both fear and desire in dream fail to leave the trace we would expect. Immediately upon the dream, still held by it, we are overwhelmed by events which, if they were real, would shake our lives; a few hours later it is as if nothing has happened and we are left only with a fading trace of something not necessarily a part of what we think our lives "are" at all. So the dream is not in fact an addition to memory, but a manipulation of it, a collaging of disparate features into a tableau. And once we are out of the dream's grasp the memories become as distant as they actually are. Their renewal, the new projection and immediacy of the dream, is an illusion. This is where we know that the dream takes images from all over our time and forms a unit of them which is outside our time; if it were within, its events would retain the force of current realities. The waking mind translates the dream into an illusion of time for the purposes of transmission, but we remain deeply unconvinced of the reality of these experiences, once we are out of the dream's power. This is very like reading a novel.

It is something we do without experiencing it; something we know without believing it. Whatever emotional turmoil we awaken into we know that it isn't real. We are quite cheated into strong responses, and it can only be ourselves who trick us in this way into responding to a fiction. What I've called the "dream invasion" of reality is of course precisely the setting up of fictions as working contexts, whether we're talking about the seducer's beady eye or the House of Commons (possibly the most aggressive school dormitory in the land). And there is the dream-fiction of the self clad in future uniform which we call ambition. But I think the most interesting emergent point from all this is not just that these more or less delusive states exist, and further certain kinds of act by way of maintaining their own existence, but that at the same time they are not believed in by their agents. There can be no actual belief, no certainty beyond episodic impulses, and only really a kind of option, a deliberate disregard of non-dream for the duration of the episode. In the cases of prime ministers, Popes, post-structuralists and hardened criminals this partialised pseudo-belief may be extended to cover all or most of an adult life, but that does not alter its nature. It is a theatre. It is the dream theatre which makes almost everybody including Nazi chancellors believe that what they do is for the good, and not just for their own good. Nothing within experience proves them wrong except the results, probably long-term, of their acts and the accumulated knowledge in the hearts of others which may predict such results. Tolstoy declared (in *The Death of Ivan Ilyich*) that what shows the dream theatre within which lives are constructed to be a makeshift hideaway is its final cancellation at the moment of death. But this is an incommunicable event and it is Tolstoy's theatrical dream to propose it. So there are grades of theatrical dream, more or less informed by world and thought.

If the dream is fiction, theatre, script, than it must be a language. Must it? The dream is not a language but a linguistic structure. Structure is where language fails, the doubt about language. It is where you say, "tree", and somebody, across some distance, hears "nature" or "wood" or "three" or "noun"... The dream is a structure, an anti-language, because there can be no actual transfer, no distance covered, no other reached. The communication is of self with self, and can utter only what is already in the possession of the self. In thought or meditation language may be said to be deployed before a fictive non-self representing the world; in dream this figure is a disguised self. In thought language has a content which is prepared as a rehearsal for transmission; indeed new content can be created in thought by setting the known against resistance as two contrary formats of memory. But the dream has no real content—it steals its content from our lives and none of it has any real presence. So there can be no resolution and no creation. The only operative resistance in dream is the *resistance to* dream from its exterior in awakening, the reduction of dream to a linear construct and our willed resistance to its apparent content, our worried attempts to penetrate the implications of its obscurities and concealments. These conflicts take place outside the dream itself. Even what I have called the dream's "bounty" is meaningless except as the awake mind's conscious deployment of matter presented to it in dream, whether this process is seen as a dream/awaking collaboration or as a contest.

Freud optimistically proposed that we can overcome dream's self deceit, that a language of lies and evasions must, on investigation, come to reveal the truth, that this deceit is no more than an arrest pending a final and natural revelation (which can be indefinitely postponed) of what would otherwise remain for ever hidden. That would be a victory over dream. But to gain this we have to allow dream all the benefit of the doubt, to assume that it inhabits and represents in its clumsy and deceptive way an actually existing department of the mind otherwise closed to us, of which we can have no certainty; and there is finally nothing to guarantee that the explanations and prophesies we gain are anything but further dream structures set to protect us from world and thought. For language is a subtle, vegetative entity which is no sooner forced out of the dream than it starts to find its way back. A new vocabulary and a new understanding are made, which at once start to become factors of another dream-invasion, retracting into an inhabitable theatre, a facility. Language as a tool of understanding requires constant sharpening on alterity, which dream-analysis, as an event focused into the self, is not equipped to perform. So the art of reading lies in the exemplary re-creation of language's primary emergence from dream in the act of discovery, crossed with its established access to objectivity, otherwise it is already a limit as soon as it is transmitted.

Is not poetry one of the places where the creation of form, the achievement of truth, and the effulgence of language as an ever newness, are all the same thing?

Breaking the dream we complete it, transcend it, and transcend ourselves. Dreams and other worlds are mirror tricks. "After the first death there is no other". The whole dream is an instantaneous vacancy, a moment containing absolutely nothing, not within a life. The polished sides of this empty sphere are made to reflect us back to ourselves, fragmented and distorted into an experience which we then plot forth as a series of events. So all we see in the dream is the self with the world behind it. It is an anti-linguistic falsity to recall or tell anything of the dream at all, because there was nothing there. The whole narrative is a pack of lies, as we recognise soon after we emerge from it. But the central untruth of the dream world, the central false image glanced off a vacancy, and the central corroding force of dream-invasion, which is when the structures of dream are wrapped round our perception of reality, is that the world is an event of the self, and that what we are is an "identity". Nobody is an identity. Identity is how we are recognised by others, each differently, like people in novels. Identity is how we are identified; it is our number. Everyone knows that the self is not an *idem*, not a unit, not a singularity fixed in a sphere but a repertoire and interplay of perceptual positions advanced into the world.

Breaking this mirror we view the real world behind it. That is, to complete the mirror into a doorway, and step through it into a world which is not previsioned. Beyond the dream we create our percepts in collaboration (or, again, contestation) with the world.

Everyone goes around wrapped in a "dream". No one escapes this condition, the habitual coloration or interpretation of presence in relation to the self's history and ambitions. Only goals which are not defined from within (from the dream) have a chance of partially escaping the dream. The perpetrators of the mass killing camps I'm sure thought that they did what they did for the best, and not necessarily for their own gain. The good result is beyond the loving or relating self to determine; it must be fixed by a wisdom from outside, of long standing in a reliable history of process. Or a single moral thunderbolt that shatters the entire institutional dream sphere, but where does that come from if not from history itself?

The night's total dream contains all we could want as of ourselves, but as a separate thing, divorced from the realities which it colours and distorts in the day, and its goal-orientation is revealed as a perspective of loss. Dream-laden goals are goals pulled down into failure, they are revenge goals.

The whole of a life up to the point of experience forms the stage of the total dream, where personal existence is read as an inhabited enclosure (with a pin-hole in it) reflected in a spherical mirror, so that we can only view one (curved, receding) facet at a time, and what we are is thus in the process of being lost. There is no escaping this personal dream, behind us during the day, in front of us during sleep, as a fictional place which we inhabit and which conditions our thoughts and acts. It is our language. But it is not everything. It is as if we carry an untruth around with us all the time, wearing it like a pair of spectacles. But what spectacles do is focus, and in order to focus on one thing in the world it is necessary to blur or distort everything else. This must be where "dream" and "real" become coeval, bearing each their proper and perhaps equal portion in the composition of necessity. It is here in the margins of perception that the dream stands in the day as the presence of a wholeness and an elsewhere, supportive or enhancing or corrective to our focus as long as it participates in sequentiality, as long as the focusing is not fixated. The focusing sequence, liberated from dream but never forgetful of it, is our work, our uniqueness, our being human.

Is not intimacy the correlation of two of these precise foci enclosed in dream? And is not the dream surround the enabling factor, where the transition can begin?

It is strange that we need this fiction in order to gain our truth. But we do, because there is something in it which is essential, some format for the renewal or furtherance of the single truth we ever know at one time, something urging a circumspection by which we progress into duration. So we hold truth wrapped in untruth. Or "uncertainty" as a *framework* to belief (Kierkegaard's idea).

It should seemingly be more straightforward. Good acts are plain enough by their good consequences, out there in the world, if you wait long enough. Yet there is some gravitational pull back from the offer of self into the act, there is a blurred surround to the act, a doubt, or even a disbelief in it, which refers to a wholeness, a great or unlimited extent of possibility. The act is good but very small scale and so fails to feed the dream. Should the dream's appetite be allowed to swamp good acts in this way? Isn't it much more important to learn to distrust the head signifier, the authority which takes acts up into the unbroken large-scale dream and offers to guarantee their benefit on a world scale? Acts of destruction and brutality which are repugnant to perform are declared necessary and delightful because they advance something much bigger: race, nation, creed, "our way of life", democracy and freedom, all these vast wholesale fictions. Haven't we finished yet with these tribal nightmares? Haven't the hypocrisies behind their declarations stood sufficiently revealed? Aren't the good act, and good will itself, both robbed by them of their value, their "own reward"?

"Dream" is at least three things. It is the actual dreaming to do with sleep; it is an anti-realistic force in our perception of the world and the self, but it is also a force of transcendence. And each of these is a metaphor for each of the other.

The point, again, is that dream refers us to a whole. Even the shabby remnants of self-imagery that we recall at the end of a night's sleep do, in their yearning demand for a completion, refers us to the utterly complete and entire compaction of the person in sleep, and to the wholeness of the moment. All the distortions of what I've called dream invasion derive from something like a premature referral to a whole, a place we seek to inhabit in a state of wholeness, but which is not an actuality. The particular is referred to a whole which effectively conceals it; the dream trespasses onto the focus and colours, clouds, bends, directs, inverts, buries it... The work focus, the engagement with the real, like the good act, is the definer at the centre and if it is obscured the whole structure becomes meaningless. The realised dream, the true wholeness, should be not merely enriched by the good act, but constituted of it, in all its percepts and histories.

Wholes are dangerous things and easily fallen into. They need constant testing against actualities or they become figments. That testing of the structure is the function of the work focus and its justification. The particular and the larger concepts construct each other.

And if the dream is a theatre of explanation referring to a whole; if the waking dream transcends the bodily sensations which disrupt sleep; if the dream covers the realities of the sleep-waking contest by projecting them into a whole sphere which we glimpse as fragmented narrative when sleep ends... if worldness itself is an expression of the wholeness of the moment, which is reduced to a narrative in order to effect a transition of states... Hamlet's question than gains a new strength. If the moment of waking sets up such a sphere, what does the moment of death do, and how do we live it?

For it occurs to me that we always enter death from a state of sleep, however microscopic the duration of the sleep might be; also that it might be true that we always die at a point where the continuation of bodily existence becomes an impossibility, however slow the transition of such a decision may be.

Isn't there then going to be a dream full of the whole of a life, which is the dream we enter at death? – isn't that dream then going to *be* the whole life? Isn't the very wholeness which the waking mind abhors and rescues us from by its literary devices, death? Isn't death's moment the only actual whole there is, the actual consummation which includes all possibilities? And isn't this new dream of life going to be the one dream which will not be interrupted, and cannot leave an aching void behind it, but will be the complete dream with its beginning, middle, and end, however broken it looks to those left behind? Isn't this where we start to inhabit the moment?

www.ingramcontent.com/pod-product-compliance
Lightning Source LLC
Chambersburg PA
CBHW022008160426
43197CB00007B/338